Contexts in Literature

Shakespeare on Stage

WEEK LOAN

Stephen Siddall

Series editor: Adrian Barlow

CAMBRIDGE
UNIVERSITY PRESS

CAMBRIDGE UNIVERSITY PRESS
Cambridge, New York, Melbourne, Madrid, Cape Town, Singapore,
São Paulo, Delhi

Cambridge University Press
The Edinburgh Building, Cambridge CB2 8RU, UK

www.cambridge.org
Information on this title: www.cambridge.org/9780521716185

First published 2008

Printed in the United Kingdom at the University Press, Cambridge

A catalogue record for this publication is available from the British Library

ISBN 978-0-521-71618-5 paperback

Editorial management: Gill Stacey

ACKNOWLEDGEMENTS

The author and publishers wish to thank the following for permission to use copyright
material:

Guardian News and Media Ltd for Michael Billington 'Macbeth seizes Moscow in a
coup de theatre: Macbeth Minerva, Chichester 4/5', the *Guardian*, 4.6.07. Copyright
© Guardian News & Media Ltd 2007; and extracts from Michael Billington 'King Lear
Review', the *Guardian*, 13.7.90. Copyright © Guardian News & Media Ltd 1990; and
Susannah Clapp 'Is this a classic I see before me?', the *Guardian*, 10.6.07. Copyright
© Guardian News & Media Ltd 2007

Every effort has been made to reach copyright holders; the publishers would like to
hear from anyone whose rights they have unknowingly infringed.

Cover photograph from the National Theatre's production of *Hamlet* in 2000.
© Donald Cooper/Photostage.

Contents

Introduction

Shakespeare's working life in the theatre started around 1590 and lasted for nearly 25 years. He was a poet, an actor and a remarkable playwright. His reputation since then has been so spectacular that we can be misled into thinking of him as a genius working in inspired solitude. But theatre is practical, collaborative and commercial. Shakespeare was a shrewd businessman in a flourishing company. He knew how to work with the many talents around him; he knew what types of play were popular; he could exploit the facilities and traditions of different (indoor and outdoor) playhouses. Staging a play is a communal activity: a group of artists gathers to create and express the play; a larger group is persuaded to attend as audience. The act of communication that follows can be complicated, exciting, joyful, inspiring, alarming – sometimes even dangerous. Therefore a play's script is generally more vibrant in performance than in its reading as a text.

Plays emerge from the historical, cultural and social influences of their birth, and so it is helpful to audiences who see his plays 400 years later to know about Shakespeare's world. However, England between 1580 and 1620 gives only one period of context. This book aims to explore a wider context too. Like all great artists, Shakespeare has had a rich afterlife. His plays have been constantly performed since his death in 1616. His friend, the playwright Ben Jonson, believed that 'He was not of an age, but for all time.'

The plays are not simply repeated. They are re-interpreted, re-expressed, sometimes even rewritten, often according to the beliefs of the times when they are performed. For example, a 1980 feminist production of *Much Ado About Nothing* in a small studio space may feel a very different play from a lavish Victorian version at the height of the male-dominated British Empire. A Marxist *Richard II* will present the monarchy differently from Shakespeare's company in the 1590s or an elegantly poetic 1930s production.

This 'fate' that comes upon a work of art (or 'rich variety', depending on how we judge the changes) is more striking for a play than is likely for the afterlife of a poem, novel, painting, symphony or sculpture. A play in performance requires more varied types of collaboration: from actors, directors, designers, lighting, theatre spaces. It also embodies flesh-and-blood encounters – thus audiences may respond to the appearance and personalities of the actors, as well as to the words they speak and the stories they tell.

These complex relationships of plays to their many contexts may seem bewildering. You may feel that all treatments of Shakespeare can become equally justified. But actors and directors constantly make judgements about what they want the plays to communicate. It is right that audiences and performance critics do the same. This book aims to help you with your own informed judgements, too.

How this book is organised

Part 1: The theatre in Shakespeare's lifetime
Part 1 examines the stage conditions and styles of playing that influenced Shakespeare's writing.

Part 2: Shakespeare in performance after 1660
Part 2 considers Shakespeare's reputation and how this has affected productions of his plays and approaches to acting up to the present day.

Part 3: Critical approaches
Part 3 outlines some of the critical and theoretical perspectives that influence the ways in which directors and actors may approach the playing of Shakespeare.

Part 4: Extracts and performance issues
Part 4 contains passages from the plays and discusses performance issues.

Part 5: How to write about Shakespeare on stage
Part 5 offers guidelines for those for whom this book is chiefly intended: students studying Shakespeare as part of an advanced course in Literature or Theatre Studies.

Part 6: Resources
This part contains a chronology, together with guidance on further reading, films, videos and websites, and a glossary and index. (Terms which appear in the glossary are highlighted in bold type when they first appear in the main text.)

At different points throughout the book, and chiefly in Part 4, there are tasks and issues for discussion designed to help the reader reflect on ideas discussed in the text.

All extracts from the plays are taken from the New Cambridge Shakespeare series.

1 | The theatre in Shakespeare's lifetime

- What was the theatre of Shakespeare's day like?

- Who performed, and who watched, plays in the Elizabethan theatre?

- How were the plays acted?

- What mattered more: hearing or seeing a play?

The playhouse

Much has been researched, guessed and written about what an Elizabethan playhouse looked like. The new Globe in Southwark (1995) has been built to imitate Shakespeare's Globe of 1599 and to revive the physical conditions for his plays. It would be a mistake, however, to think that there was only one type of playhouse. In 1576 James Burbage built the first permanent public playhouse in London. He called it 'The Theatre' because this was a dignified Roman word connected with oratory and would help in the marketing of his plays.

Burbage was also aiming to continue the loose and varied traditions of the travelling players, who had no fixed home and were prepared to play whatever and wherever seemed profitable. Often they played beneath the outdoor galleries of inn-yards, but they might also be found in market squares, village greens, private gardens and inside large houses. Travelling players had to be versatile – even after 1576 most had no permanent playhouse to play in. For example, in London in the 1590s there were regular outbreaks of plague and other infections during the summer months. Then playhouses would be closed and the players returned to the road, touring the towns and villages and performing in different types of space. And nowadays too Shakespeare's plays invite equally versatile treatment: in pubs, village halls, gardens and other spaces that are not always designed as theatres.

Drawings and other written evidence suggest that, although the public playhouses of London varied in many details, there were a few basic and repeated requirements. J.L. Styan summarises these in his book *Shakespeare's Stagecraft*:

- a tight enclosing auditorium

- a projecting platform almost as deep as it was wide

- two **upstage** entrances onto the platform

- at least one balcony

The circular or polygonal building hemmed in the audience around three sides of the platform, so that everyone was very close to the action, whether standing in the yard around the platform or sitting in greater comfort in the balconies. Audiences were mixed: apprentices, lawyers from the Inns of Court, fashionable young men and women. Though there would be noise and movement during performance, they were certainly not the lewd rabble that hostile **Puritan** critics described them as.

The platform was raised, ensuring clear vision for audiences in the yard, and allowing a trapdoor for surprising entrances and special effects such as ghosts or Ophelia's grave in *Hamlet*. Generally, actors appeared at the upstage doors in the facade (decorated screen) but processions might pass through the yard. An actor could cover the large distance down towards the audience to command the centre of the building for soliloquies and other intimate scenes. The balcony was an extra asset; it could add another dimension to the scenes below:

- In *Richard II* the king self-dramatises his fall to 'the base court' where Northumberland stands beneath him: 'Down, down I come, like glistering Phaëton.'

- Cleopatra, taking refuge in her monument, has the dying Antony carried 'aloft' to her.

- Richard of Gloucester (planning to be King Richard III) takes part in a tableau to impress the London crowds: he pretends to be a devout Christian by holding a prayer book and standing between two bishops.

But these pictorial moments above the platform were not extra decoration: the actors entered to begin or continue part of the play's action. Telling the story was their main purpose.

The Globe

Burbage's company, The Lord Chamberlain's Men, occupied the land for The Theatre on a 21-year lease. In 1598 that lease had expired. It was a particularly frosty winter, but the company dismantled the building, carried the timbers across the River Thames and settled on the south bank in Southwark. There they built a new playhouse near to The Rose, where their rivals, The Lord Admiral's Men, played. Such was their confidence that they named their new home 'The Globe'. The new title, another marketing decision like 'The Theatre', referred not just to its circular shape, but also to the purpose and scale of its enterprise. The playhouse mirrored the world; stories of all people and events could be staged there. The stage imitating the world or, as Jaques put it in *As You Like It*, the world being a type of stage, was not a new metaphor. It caught exactly the adventurous spirit of the age, the drama and passion of spectacular lives. The Elizabethan courtier Sir

Walter Raleigh lived such a life and understood the metaphor. He was a statesman, historian and discoverer as well as being a fine poet:

> What is our life? A play of passion.
> And what our mirth but music of division?
> Our mother's wombs the tiring houses be
> Where we are drest for this short comedy.
> Heaven the judicious sharp spectator is
> Who sits and marks what here we do amiss.
> The graves that hide us from the searching sun
> Are like drawn curtains when the play is done.
> Thus playing post we to our latest rest,
> And then we die, in earnest, not in jest.

The Globe was ready within six months for the busy summer season of 1599. It was large and well-equipped. Like most playhouses, the Globe was 'sumptuous' and 'gorgeous', according to some Puritan critics. Some of the woodwork was carved and some painted to look like Italian marble. The canopy above the platform was painted as 'the heavens' with sun, moon and stars. It was designed to excite and delight audiences, even before the play started. But its life was short. Like all wooden buildings, it was vulnerable and was burnt down in 1613, when a cannon fired flaming material into its roof during a performance of *Henry VIII*. A second Globe was erected in 1614 and demolished in 1644.

1599 was also a year of great achievement for Shakespeare. He was by then the most experienced and talented playwright in London. He helped to supervise the building of the Globe, and the year saw the first performances of *Julius Caesar*, *As You Like It* and *Henry V.*

Shakespeare and The Lord Chamberlain's Men were so successful at The Globe that they were honoured by James I and after 1603 were known as The King's Men. In 1608, needing an indoor playhouse, they took over The Blackfriars to supplement The Globe and to provide a winter home. Blackfriars had once been a monastery, then from 1576 was used as a private playhouse for one of the children's companies (see page 29, below) and subsequently became a public playhouse. It was smaller than The Globe, seating about 500. More indoor playhouses began to be built at this time, charging higher entrance prices and providing more comfort and refinement. Such playhouses led gradually towards the late 17th-century **proscenium** theatres with their greater interest in spectacle. In The Globe the company aimed to 'play to the gallery', where the wealthier, better educated audience would be sitting. In the smaller Blackfriars such audiences were very close to the stage and this invited a quieter, more intimate style of playing (similar to today's theatres where the most expensive seats are in the stalls).

The King's Men were already performing at court; they were a versatile company and Shakespeare was used to writing for different types of playhouse. The Blackfriars had a music-room in a curtained gallery above the stage for the original boys' companies. These companies included trained musicians, both choristers and instrumentalists. Sometimes plays performed there had been preceded by a concert. It is unlikely that Shakespeare wrote any plays exclusively for Blackfriars, but his last plays, written after 1608, like *The Tempest*, *Pericles* and *The Winter's Tale*, are chiefly mysterious **romances** that depend heavily on different types of music.

The masque

After about 1610, playhouse history included performances at court, notably the **masque**. This was an elaborate entertainment that would include song and dance to decorate a fanciful story loaded with **allegorical** meaning. It was often staggeringly expensive. It was also used as part of court display to impress visiting dignitaries. The masque looked ahead to the development of opera, which also demands scenery and complicated stage effects behind a proscenium arch. Ben Jonson (see page 13, below) wrote several masques in partnership with the great architect Inigo Jones. Jonson complained that the scenery drew more applause than the poetry; this indicates how spectacle was replacing both language and robust interaction with an audience.

Shakespeare's *The Tempest* includes three moments that are strongly influenced by masque:

- Ariel's fantastical banquet for the 'three men of sin'

- the masque of goddesses to celebrate the betrothal of Ferdinand and Miranda

- the lovers' game of chess for the on-stage audience of lords.

Some later revivals of *The Tempest*, especially in the late 17th century, have treated it more as a masque than a play (see page 46).

The companies

Early in Queen Elizabeth's reign the government wanted to reduce the threat of political and religious unrest. One measure in 1572 was to encourage people to remain in their locality. It was called the Act for Restraining Vagabonds. This badly affected troupes of players, who needed to be constantly travelling between towns and villages searching for audiences. The Act compelled the more talented players to gain security by attaching themselves to noble families. They would then perform in large households on special occasions. Shakespeare drew on this tradition in *Much Ado About Nothing* when Don Pedro and his soldiers have just arrived in Leonato's house. The party on their first night begins with the soldiers masked, pretending to be a group of players, 'invading' the house, probably with a robust performance like a sword-dance. When they have made their noisy contribution, they dance with the ladies.

Even though companies wore their patron's livery (uniform), they were also highly commercial and continued to perform popular plays for the general public. The major companies settled in London in new playhouses that became their permanent homes. The Theatre, managed by James Burbage, was the first of these in 1576, but protests from city authorities forced the company to build it just outside the city's northern walls. The Theatre was so successful that soon more playhouses were built, eventually within the city, and permanent London companies competed for audiences and for the best players. Each one also required a constant supply of new plays. Thus hardship followed by commercial activity helped to bring about the great burst of play-writing between 1580 and 1640.

After the 1570s companies gradually improved their status, thanks to enthusiastic audiences and support from nobility and crown. They took their titles from their patrons: The Lord Chamberlain's Men (which included Shakespeare and Burbage), The Lord Admiral's Men, The Queen's Men, The Earl of Leicester's Men. When King James I came to the throne in 1603, he developed further the tradition of players performing at court, and so The Lord Chamberlain's Men, the leading company at the time, gained extra dignity in becoming The King's Men.

Much of the information about the companies comes from Philip Henslowe's diaries, written in the early 1590s. Henslowe was a financier who saw that profits could be made from flourishing playhouses, as well as from brothels and other places of entertainment. He went into partnership with Edward Alleyn, London's leading player, and they were shrewd enough to sign up the great playwright, Christopher Marlowe. This powerful association made them, as The Lord Admiral's Men, London's pre-eminent company. But by the mid-1590s The Lord Chamberlain's Men had overtaken them.

Each company had a core of about eight to twelve leading players, known as 'sharers', who took the financial risks and expected to make handsome profits. This small number of players was not enough to stage plays whose cast lists might stretch to 35 named parts, even with doubling the parts. Hired men had to be brought in to double most of the smaller roles, and boys to play the women and the younger servants.

Plays were commissioned and written rapidly. Most were given only a few performances, though the more popular ones might be revived a few years later. Henslowe records that in one period of 25 days, 15 different plays were presented at his theatre. Given the length of some (*Richard III* is over 4000 lines) the leading players, like Alleyn and Richard Burbage (James's son) must have developed prodigious memories. Rehearsal was not the thoughtful, analytic, time-consuming process expected from today's major productions. Each play was hurried onto the stage. Performing it depended heavily on the players' technique and experience and a readiness to improvise. For example, there would be almost formulaic staging of court scenes and processions, with each player knowing his character's position in the social hierarchy.

Audiences flocked to the playhouses for the sense of occasion, for vigorously told stories and to see the star performers. Clowns like Richard Tarleton, Robert Armin and Will Kempe (see pages 31–32, below) established a lively rapport with their fans. Performances, with up to 3000 people packed tightly round the three-sided stage, could be vibrant occasions. By the mid-1590s players of passionate tragedy had become the new stars: Richard Burbage was the lead actor in The Lord Chamberlain's Men for several years. Shakespeare wrote parts like Richard III, Macbeth and Othello for him, and perhaps Lear and Antony too.

Popular plays and playwrights

When Shakespeare first came to London to begin his career as a player in the late 1580s, John Lyly was the most popular and prolific playwright. His elegant artificial romances, many written specially for the children's companies (see page 29, below) influenced Shakespeare in writing his romantic comedies: *Love's Labours Lost*, *The Two Gentlemen of Verona*, *As You Like It*, *A Midsummer Night's Dream*. Most of Lyly's plays include: girls dressed as boys; wit-contests between lovers; clowns echoing the play's **themes** in their subplot; an idyllic pastoral setting; journeys, songs, coincidence and fantastical events. All this sounds very Shakespearean, but Shakespeare was shrewdly exploiting what Lyly had already made popular.

Thomas Kyd (1558–1594) is a more mysterious figure. His great achievement was to develop revenge tragedy, one of the most popular genres of the age. His play *The Spanish Tragedy* was an often-revived theatrical triumph. It includes a ghost, madness, disguise, deceit, a play-within-a-play and a bloodthirsty conclusion. Shakespeare understood the value of this mixture when in 1593 he wrote his first Roman play *Titus Andronicus*, also a popular and much-revived work, and then in 1600 his own version of *Hamlet*. Kyd may also have written a play about Hamlet (now lost).

Christopher Marlowe (1564–1593) led a notorious and dangerous life. Many characters in his plays seem to express his own subversive tendencies: they can be violent, blasphemous, rebellious and highly assertive. Like Shakespeare, he was born in 1564, but had a more academic background and worked as a spy in Queen Elizabeth's secret service. Writing for The Lord Admiral's Men in the early 1590s, he was an obvious rival for Shakespeare and The Lord Chamberlain's Men. In just six explosive years of playwriting he produced memorable tragedies, boldly laced with strands of grotesque **farce**. His *Dr Faustus* and *The Jew of Malta* were two of the most popular plays in the period and were continually revived until 1642, when Puritan objections to immoral and subversive plays led to parliament closing the theatres. Marlowe's promising career was brutally ended: he died in a violent brawl when only 29.

Ben Jonson (1572–1637) is considered to be another rival. Jonson was meticulous, more evidently an intellectual than Shakespeare and not especially popular in the public theatres. He wrote for indoor theatres and eventually joined with the architect Inigo Jones to create expensive allegorical masques for the court. However, critics later in the 17th century admired him more than Shakespeare, particularly for his satirical city comedies, *Volpone* and *The Alchemist*. Jonson himself recognised Shakespeare's genius, but also felt that Shakespeare's writing was a little rough and that he could have taken pains to revise and edit.

After 1610 the most performed playwright was John Fletcher. His play *The Tamer Tamed* was an answer to the male dominance of Shakespeare's *The Taming of the Shrew* and was far more popular. When parliament closed the theatres in 1642, actors trying to re-establish themselves chose plays by Fletcher and not Shakespeare. Writing in 1647 the poet Sir John Denham, noted for the elegance of his style, praised Jonson for 'Art', Shakespeare for 'Nature', but Fletcher's 'Wit' combined the virtues of the other two. Being university educated, he was thought to surpass Shakespeare, the rustic provincial. And Fletcher was again more popular when Charles II became king and the theatres re-opened in 1660.

Shakespeare's own most performed plays were *Henry IV Part 1*, *Richard III*, *Pericles*, *Hamlet*, *Richard II*, *Romeo and Juliet*. All of these plays, except *Pericles*, were written before 1600, towards the middle of his career. Three history plays are among these six but, surprisingly, no comedies and nothing from the group of mature tragedies – *Macbeth*, *Othello*, *King Lear* – which appear so frequently on today's exam syllabuses and are often described as his highest achievement.

A playwright was rarely working alone. The play was generally fashioned on stage with the players and often written in collaboration. Beaumont and Fletcher wrote as a well-known partnership, and Shakespeare joined with Fletcher at the end of his career to write *Cardenio*, *Henry VIII* and *Two Noble Kinsmen*. Even when a play was written, it was often revised and adapted by someone else, especially if it was popular enough to be revived. Thomas Middleton made significant changes to *Macbeth*. Indeed, most early plays, first written as continuous action, needed adapting to include intervals.

Where did Shakespeare find his material?

Elizabethan playwrights were not expected to be original, in the sense of having to create everything themselves from scratch. In fact, the modern meaning of the word 'originality' didn't appear in the English language until the late 18th century. The Elizabethans valued imitation in education, literature and popular culture, and they enjoyed familiar stories and genres, especially in classical writers like Ovid, Horace and Seneca. But Shakespeare's contemporary Ben Jonson condemned imitation that was merely slavish. He believed the poet must 'be able to convert the substance or riches of another poet to his own use ... Not as a creature that swallows what it takes in crude, raw and undigested, but that feeds with an appetite, and hath a stomach to concoct, divide, and turn all into nourishment.'

Like most of his contemporaries, Shakespeare was a sort of literary magpie: he found fragments of useful material from his reading and from watching other plays. As an actor, he played only smaller roles, but the company employed him to rework and update earlier plays. He was alert to topical events and a close observer of both London and rural life. An exasperated contemporary playwright, Robert Greene, criticised him as being an impudent upstart, lacking both the sophistication of court and the academic distinction of university. But some critics believe that it was Shakespeare's rural Warwickshire background, combined with his robust London life, that made him especially versatile as a playwright. Note, for example, how easily comedies and romances (for instance, *As You Like It* or *The Winter's Tale*) use the interplay of court and country scenes.

Most of his plays were based on one prominent source, a story or an old play, that could supply the main characters and events. None are exclusively reworkings of this one source; they all depend on other influences too.

Prose romances

Shakespeare used material from prose romances for his comedies. The story of *As You Like It* comes from a popular English source, Thomas Lodge's *Rosalynde*, published in 1590. Lodge got *his* material from a vigorous romance poem from the Middle Ages. Shakespeare also used two stories from *Hecatommithi*, a collection of 100 stories published in 1565 by Giraldi Cinthio, an Italian author, to give him the basis of *Measure for Measure* and *Othello*. Some stories gave Shakespeare valuable but slighter amounts of material: Golding's translation of Ovid's *Metamorphoses* influenced *The Tempest* and *A Midsummer Night's Dream*. Another important influence was the infamous handbook for political success: Niccolò Machiavelli's *The Prince* (1532). Machiavelli explains how to gain and to keep power without being bound by conscience or other moral concerns. The '**machiavel**' even became a character on stage and his attitudes merged with those of the medieval Vice (see page 32, below). Shakespeare's histories and tragedies include several such prominent characters: Richard III (see extract in Part 4, page 90), Iago in *Othello* and Edmund in *King Lear*.

Old plays

John Lyly's elegant romances in the 1580s influenced Shakespeare's early writing. Lyly's *Gallathea* provided material for the plot of *A Midsummer Night's Dream*, though Shakespeare drew on other non-dramatic material too. **Revenge tragedy** was another genre guaranteed to bring commercial success. Shakespeare was familiar with a play about Hamlet, performed in the 1580s but since lost. It is thought that Thomas Kyd also wrote a play about Hamlet, and, alert to popular taste, Shakespeare wrote his *Hamlet* in 1599. Successful plays performed by rival companies could inspire a new play. *The Merchant of Venice*, sometimes entitled 'The Jew of Venice', was in some ways an answer to Marlowe's *The Jew of Malta*, as well as borrowing some characters and events from an Italian novella called *Il pecorone*. However, Shakespeare challenged Marlowe as well as using him: he reduced the grotesque and farcical aspects of Barabas, Marlowe's hero-villain, and, while accepting the anti-Jew prejudice of the time, made his own Shylock a subtler personality.

History

As a commercial playwright, Shakespeare responded to the popularity of plays about history, or **Chronicle Plays**, as they were known. Through eight plays that he wrote during the 1590s, he told a dramatised story of the English monarchy in the hundred years from Richard II to the death of Richard III in 1485. These plays are based chiefly on the chronicles of Edward Hall and Ralph Holinshed. But neither the two chroniclers nor Shakespeare himself are as accurate as modern historians might wish. All are biased in the interests of propaganda, especially in supporting the Tudor dynasty, which had ruled England since 1485. The plays take further inventive liberties: they make important moments vividly theatrical and they speculate on the private thoughts and feelings of the main public characters.

By Shakespeare's time history plays had partly replaced medieval morality plays in putting the nation rather than an 'Everyman' figure at the moral centre of the drama. In a commercial sense history provided an easily available source of plots for the Elizabethan theatre managers, who needed a constant supply of new plays. History was also considered to be **didactic**: the mistakes and successes of the past provided lessons that could instruct audiences. This was a useful argument against Puritan complaints that the theatre was immoral. Shakespeare wrote about Roman history too, so that of his 37 plays a heavy proportion of 14 are history plays. A case could also be argued for adding the Scottish *Macbeth*, and the play set in ancient Britain, *Cymbeline*.

Topical events and conditions

There is no play by Shakespeare that is substantially based on the political events of his own time: a company would not engage so thoroughly in dangerous controversy. However, most plays allude to contemporary tastes, concerns and events. In Act 5 the Chorus in *Henry V* compares the king's triumphant return to England to a 'conquering Caesar' and, more topically, to the Earl of Essex returning from wars in Ireland:

> Were now the general of our gracious empress,
> (As in good time he may) from Ireland coming,
> Bringing rebellion broachèd on his sword,
> How many would the peaceful city quit
> To welcome him?

At the time this must have seemed a shrewd piece of flattery, but a few months later Essex mobilised his army against the queen and marched towards London. To persuade Londoners to support him, Essex's publicity organisation paid for The Lord Chamberlain's Men to perform Shakespeare's *Richard II*, which tells the story of a bold military hero replacing a weak monarch. This example of a play's topical relevance proved deeply embarrassing to the company when Essex was arrested. Sometimes plays aimed to challenge the mystique of the monarchy: whereas Queen Elizabeth presented herself as a distant icon (Gloriana, the Virgin Queen) for her subjects, playwrights presented kings as troubled individuals who may struggle with their public role.

In *Henry V* the king, in disguise, visits his soldiers the night before Agincourt. When a common soldier challenges his policy in France, the king tries to reply without revealing his identity. We may feel that his arguments are evasive and weaker than the soldier's. In *Richard II*, when the king is about to be deposed, the Bishop of Carlisle protests:

> What subject can give sentence on his king,
> And who sits here that is not Richard's subject?

Shakespeare may appear to support traditional monarchy, but he also encouraged an audience to feel ambivalent about Richard's conduct as king. Here, through Carlisle, Shakespeare has encouraged audiences to debate the controversial question about the status and powers of a king. That issue dominated the 1630s and 1640s, a turbulent period in English history which reached a climax in 1649 when Charles I was executed.

In the 1590s the country felt unstable. Many of Shakespeare's plays draw attention to these unsettled feelings in a rapidly expanding London:

- the future of the crown after Elizabeth's death

- suspicion of foreigners

- spying and anxiety about Catholic plots

- court corruption and intrigue

- the rise of a new wealthy class challenging the traditional aristocracy

- plague and poor harvests

- rising crime

- the authority of the father in his family

- restless younger sons, who were well educated but who felt dispossessed because they would not inherit the family property or fortune.

▶ Which of these social and political problems appear in any of the plays you know?

Comparing source material with the play

Some critics believe that Shakespeare's intentions become clear when comparing his source material with the play it influenced. Two striking examples of this are *Othello* and *The Winter's Tale*.

Shakespeare found the basis for *Othello* in an Italian melodramatic story by Cinthio published in 1566. Generally he kept to Cinthio's small cast of characters, but in this case he added Brabantio, the heroine's father, and Roderigo, the feckless Venetian suitor who follows Desdemona to the military barracks in Cyprus. Inventing Roderigo allowed Shakespeare, through Iago, to control the pace of his story: a slow first three acts, then a headlong rush to disaster. It also allowed him to develop the character of Iago, who rehearses villainy on Roderigo before mentally poisoning his general, Othello. The part of Iago becomes far more prominent and puzzling than in the original melodrama, and Shakespeare manages to distinguish him sharply from Othello. In Cinthio's story the two belong much more together in a sordid world of intrigue – and at the end, they both murder Desdemona.

The Winter's Tale derives from *Pandosto*, a prose romance by Robert Greene. Shakespeare invents the new characters of Paulina and Autolycus, each supplying a different type of dramatic energy. Paulina's bold feminist common sense adds to Leontes' suffering and controls the final act. Autolycus, the confident, amoral pedlar, sings of 'the red blood' which enlivens Greene's bland story of the lovers in the spring section of the story. Most significant is the fate of the wronged queen: in

Greene she dies after her trial, whereas Shakespeare preserves her for reunion and reconciliation with her family. The astonishing final scene of her supposed statue is not only a heart-stopping moment in the theatre, but it declares a rich optimism that makes Greene's story seem shallow.

▶ Compare any Shakespeare play with the story that he used as his source material. List in three columns the changes that he made: those you consider (a) slight, (b) substantial, (c) crucial.

The actor at the centre

The playwright John Webster (*c.* 1578–1632) wrote: 'Sit in a full theatre and you will think you see so many lines drawn from the circumference of so many ears, whiles the actor is the centre.' His comment indicates two crucial aspects of Elizabethan theatre: audiences went to *hear* as well as to *see* a play (see page 21, below), and the actor is more important than the scenery. In fact, in some ways the actor *is* the scenery too, in his wearing bold costume that moves with him. Behind him is the basic permanent setting, the static – though also colourful – look of the theatre itself.

Although the actor is central, the focus for all eyes and ears, he is still the servant to the audience, who are the paying customers who could (and often did, raucously) make their feelings known if the service were poor. In countless prologues and epilogues, the actor would ask for indulgence and forgiveness:

> If we shadows have offended
> Think but this, and all is mended:
> That you have but slumbered here
> While these visions did appear;
> And this weak and idle theme,
> No more yielding but a dream …

These lines from the Epilogue of *A Midsummer Night's Dream* are fittingly spoken by Puck, who has always been half in and half out of the action, a commentator and stage manager as well as player. He refers to the company as 'shadows', a very common metaphor for players. Sometimes they seem more than ordinary people when they play kings and tragic heroes, sometimes much less, since they have no purpose or substance without the great material they play. Even that material can seem a 'weak and idle theme', rather like a dream when compared with the solid substance of real life. Tom Stoppard takes the shadow/substance idea teasingly further in his play *Rosencrantz and Guildenstern Are Dead* (first performed in 1967, and derived from Shakespeare's *Hamlet*) when the First Player complains: 'Don't you see?! We're actors – we're the opposite of people!'

Macbeth reverses the accepted notion that an actor can play a hero, when in Act 5 he sees his once-heroic life as being like the hollow performance of a barnstorming player. He asks for his life's brief flame to be extinguished:

> Out, out, brief candle,
> Life's but a walking shadow, a poor player
> That struts and frets his hour upon the stage
> And then is heard no more.

Shakespeare may be hovering here between two different questions and inviting us to consider both. Is Macbeth's player 'poor' because acting is in itself as empty as a shadow, or is he a poor example of his profession because he 'struts and frets' rather than playing with more subtlety?

It is difficult at such distance in time to reconstruct styles of acting. Some critics think that Shakespeare and The Lord Chamberlain's Men required life-like discretion from their actors, compared with the bolder style of The Lord Admiral's Men, who performed Marlowe's heroic plays in the early 1590s. But probably there was great variety within a company. There was no director to impose a unity of style and no time in rehearsal to put it into effect, even if unity (or uniformity) were thought desirable. Most playwrights of the period made a virtue out of the different skills of the players and entertained an audience with variety of scene, mood and language – 'mungrell tragic-comedy', as Sir Philip Sidney saw plays that did not fit neatly into categories. But these performances in the public playhouse grew from the robust life of popular entertainment, not from the demands of highly educated theorists.

Character or stereotype?

We have come to expect character study to be the obvious entry point for appreciating a Shakespeare play. His characters can seem to have independent life, often with stories and behaviour we think we can find prior to the action of the play and unstated between the play's lines and scenes. For example, Lady Macbeth makes a comment, never mentioned again in the play, that she suckled a child. This has become important to those critics and actresses who construct a 'back-life' for her to explain her intense and unnatural behaviour as the accomplice of a murderer.

But this elaborate focus on character was not part of Shakespeare's theatre. It developed during the late 19th century and was most fully expressed by A.C. Bradley in his book *Shakespearean Tragedy* (published in 1904; see Part 2, page 58). It was then challenged by the critic L.C. Knights in his mockingly titled essay 'How many children had Lady Macbeth?' (1933). Of course, Shakespeare's characters have thoughts and feelings which we can recognise and share, but they are often there for structural reasons: the story requires them at a particular point.

In *Much Ado About Nothing* Shakespeare concentrates on the four lovers; the villain Don John is there simply to disrupt their happiness. In *Measure for Measure* Mariana first appears in Act 4 to help the Duke's plot to support Isabella against Angelo's tyranny, but audiences are not expected to explore her past relationship with Angelo beyond the bare facts that expose his selfishness. Both Don John and Mariana perform a function and also make comments that reinforce the plays' concerns. Don John is 'not of many words', whereas Benedick, the reluctant lover, is 'evermore tattling'. Mariana begs for Angelo's life with the realistic and accepting view that 'best men are moulded out of faults'.

Shakespeare's public expected to enjoy stories about kings, soldiers, lovers, clowns – in fact, stories populated by the wider society more than by the individuals within the wider society. Sometimes Shakespeare appears to forget the name he has given to his character and writes in his scripts a general term like 'Clown' or 'Braggart' instead. Early texts of *King Lear* sometimes referred to Edmund as 'Bastard', as though his specific identity mattered less than his role as a typical **malcontent**.

In 1565 Robert Edwards wrote in his prologue to *Damon and Pythias*:

> The old man is sober, the young man rash, the lover triumphing in joys,
> The matron grave, the harlot wild and full of wanton toys,
> Which all in one course they in no wise do agree:
> So correspondent to their kind their speeches ought to be.

These lines praise the playwright's habit of stereotyping, a habit 20th-century followers of Bradley would criticise for lack of character depth. In fact, comedy, which generally borders on satire, has always concentrated on '**humours**', those characteristics that broadly define types of human nature.

There are occasions when lack of stated identity can bring an advantage. If we read *Twelfth Night* we see 'Viola' named on the page as speaking her lines. But if we watch a performance neither she nor anyone else uses the name until her twin Sebastian greets her in Act 5. There is something wonderful and mysterious about Shakespeare's reticence, as though her identity can be confirmed only at this reunion. Until then she weaves through the play influencing others by her androgynous strangeness. Meeting Sebastian, her own flesh and blood, the only character who has access to her name, is the play's memorable moment, more powerful even than the coming together of lovers. It becomes even stranger when we remember that a boy-actor plays the unnamed woman, shipwrecked at the start of the play, who survives in a strange country by taking on a disguise as a boy called Cesario – a disguise which fools everyone until the moment when Sebastian greets her:

> Were you a woman – as the rest goes even –
> I should my tears let fall upon your cheek,
> And say, 'Thrice welcome, drownèd Viola.'

Hearing a play

At the beginning of *The Taming of the Shrew*, a lord and his attendants trick Christopher Sly, a tinker, into believing he is a nobleman. When he is confused by this new status, they pretend that 'too much sadness hath congealed your blood' and that his doctors 'thought it good you hear a play'. The comedy he is to 'hear' will heal his troubled mind – more through the ears than the eyes.

A player had to be physically versatile, but his most important skills were those of the orator. He had to present his story and persuade his audience. Shakespeare, through Hamlet, tells the players to 'suit the action to the word, the word to the action'. But Hamlet is not asking for naturalism as we understand the word. He wants the players to use their craft and observe what Elizabethans called **decorum**. For example, a nobleman has a higher status than a peasant, so the playwright's language for both types of character and the actors speaking the language would show this difference in status. In the early Elizabethan playhouses these aspects of presentation were more important than our priority of impersonating a character. However, by 1600, audiences also valued convincing individuality and Richard Burbage was praised equally for **rhetoric** and for characterisation.

Rhetoric

Elizabethan education paid great attention to rhetoric, the formal study of language. Politicians today employ an aspect of rhetoric when they use pattern, often in groups of three repeated words or phrases. In Shakespeare's time rhetoric was a more varied and sophisticated study, and his early plays offer the actor stretches of verse for formal delivery that are far removed from the normal language of the street. Elizabethans were used to hearing rhetoric in church, in parliament and in the law courts. Sometimes even those condemned to death remembered their early training when speaking to the crowds from the scaffold. The theatre is a public occasion too and invites verse, song, ritual and all kinds of heightened language. In *Richard II* (Act 3 Scene 3) the king is preparing for the momentous public event of resigning his crown. Listen to the shape, pattern and ceremony of these lines:

> I'll give my jewels for a set of beads,
> My gorgeous palace for a hermitage,
> My gay apparel for an almsman's gown,
> My figured goblets for a dish of wood,
> My sceptre for a palmer's walking staff,
> My subjects for a pair of carvèd saints,
> And my large kingdom for a little grave,
> A little, little grave, an obscure grave …

The first six lines anticipate the voice ascending to the sonorous echo of 'carvèd' and 'large'. Then the **antithesis** of 'large kingdom' and 'little grave' implies a climax, the balance of dignified space against the cramped destination of the 'grave'. With the final line the predictable rhythms break down and the bumpy verse ('little, little … obscure') instructs the actor to meditate on the bleak conclusion Richard is trying to accept.

Shakespeare's early plays use patterned language more obviously than those written after 1600. Sometimes the elegant balance of word against word can sound almost like a song. This has an unsettling effect in *Richard III* when Richard, confident and persuasive, is wooing Lady Anne, who hates him. In soliloquy he has just told the audience about his grotesque appearance and ruthless intentions, so this becomes a strangely warped love-scene. At the end of their scene (Act 1 Scene 2) she is almost persuaded:

ANNE	I would I knew thy heart.
RICHARD	'Tis figured in my tongue.
ANNE	I fear me both are false.
RICHARD	Then never was man true.
ANNE	Well, well, put up your sword.
RICHARD	Say then my peace is made.
ANNE	That shalt thou know hereafter.
RICHARD	But shall I live in hope?
ANNE	All men, I hope, live so.
RICHARD	Vouchsafe to wear this ring.

Then comes the turning point as Anne puts his ring on her finger, and Richard's language reverts to the regular **iambic** blank verse, but still keeps the antithesis (here triple) of word playing against word:

> Look how my ring encompasseth thy finger.
> Even so thy breast encloseth my poor heart.

The rhetoric of a more public speaker is powerfully evident in *Julius Caesar* when both Brutus and Antony become orators to persuade the Roman crowd that Caesar did or did not deserve to die. Brutus speaks in language very close to an orator's instruction book, but it feels rather chill and overformal. Antony is more flexible in his approach. He too is master of the basic techniques of persuading, but he is more skilled in manipulating emotions: he understands that crowds are not controlled by intellect alone.

Language for the actor's voice

As his career developed, Shakespeare became more free and varied in providing language for the actor's voice. He alternated between verse and prose and also used different verse forms. Within a single speech he became more adventurous, so that an actor could do more than simply present himself and his words: he could mine deep into the character's motivation and feelings. In Act 1 of *The Winter's Tale* King Leontes is obsessed with his wife's supposed adultery. As with the extract above from *Richard II*, there is repetition here and the anticipation of pattern, but the energy of deep distress and anger gives it more staccato variety:

> Is whispering nothing?
> Is leaning cheek to cheek? Is meeting noses?
> Kissing with inside lip? Stopping the career
> Of laughter with a sigh? – a note infallible
> Of breaking honesty – Horsing foot on foot?
> Skulking in corners? Wishing clocks more swift?
> Hours, minutes? Noon, midnight? And all eyes
> Blind with the pin and web but theirs – theirs only,
> That would unseen be wicked? Is this nothing?
> Why then the world and all that's in't is nothing,
> My wife is nothing, nor nothing have these nothings,
> If this be nothing.

Listen to the pattern developing in the first two lines, which is then thrown off course by a deflecting thought, then a new pace gathering up to the angry emphasis on 'theirs', then a mid-line pause after 'wicked'. The final movement becomes more frantic and impotent with the repeated 'nothings'.

Vocal contrasts

The Elizabethan playhouse entertained its audiences through variety, which included vocal contrasts. Cries of distress and calls to battle could be heard alongside quiet, intimate speaking. The structure of the open public playhouse accommodated both with equal clarity. In Act 5 of *Macbeth* the tyrant-king snarls like an animal and then, hearing of his wife's death, retreats into profound despair about the emptiness of life. The long last scene of *Othello* centres on Desdemona's bed, but public as well as private emotions are expressed there. As Emilia dies she murmurs a line or two of Desdemona's 'willow' song, reminding the audience that the two women enjoyed the most sustained and open relationship in the play. The men surrounding her seem like intruders. Then Othello picks up his weapon and the male rhetoric of war resumes. He celebrates his military past, then seems to see Desdemona at his judgement day. The resonant language of 'heaven' and 'fiends' takes him far beyond the bedchamber, ending with a sustained cry of anguish:

> O cursèd, cursèd slave! Whip me, ye devils,
> From the possession of this heavenly sight!
> Blow me about in winds! Roast me in sulphur!
> Wash me in steep-down gulfs of liquid fire!
> O, Desdemon! Dead Desdemon! Dead. O! O!

Pauses and silence

In the midst of all Shakespeare's words, a pause and even silence can also be eloquent. For most of the trial scene in *The Merchant of Venice*, Shylock is focused, clear-headed and on the way to achieving his aim. Suddenly Portia traps him and for 30 lines he makes barely a comment. She questions this long period of near-paralysis: 'Why doth the Jew pause?' Her ironic pretending not to know of his distress is part of the Christians' destruction of 'the Jew', so that his exit (from the play as well as from the scene) is a broken mutter, not the resounding climax for a leading character. In Act 5 Scene 1 of *Measure for Measure* Mariana tries to persuade Isabella to forgive the hypocrite Angelo so that the Duke may forgive him too:

> Isabel!
> Sweet Isabel, do yet but kneel by me,
> Hold up your hands, say nothing; I'll speak all.

But Isabella makes no move, so Mariana is forced into improvising a philosophy so humane that it sounds almost comic:

> They say best men are moulded out of faults,
> And for the most become much more the better
> For being a little bad: so may my husband.

Still no move.

> Oh Isabel! Will you not lend a knee?

The Duke breaks the silence:

> He dies for Claudio's death.

Eventually Isabella finds the feeling and then the words to support Mariana. This passage is wonderfully powerful in the theatre, provided the actors are bold enough to follow Shakespeare's implicit instructions about pauses. Peter Brook (see Part 2, page 68), when directing *Measure for Measure*, urged his Isabella to hold this last pause beyond what seemed acceptable: he knew that the combination of stage picture (almost tableau) and unusual silence would give space for the audience to enter into the great moral decisions that three characters have to make here.

The speaking of lines

There are no recordings of how lines were spoken in the Elizabethan theatre, so it is difficult for theatre historians to be very precise about this important aspect of playing. Hamlet asks that his lines shall be spoken 'trippingly on the tongue'. This probably refers to the musical qualities of the verse. An actor's training should equip him for some subtlety rather than the sheer volume of a town crier. Burbage's greatness as an actor lay significantly in the music of the voice:

> ... there was as much difference between him and one of our common actors as between a ballad singer who only mouths it and an excellent singer who knows all his graces and can artfully vary and modulate his voice, even to know how much breath he is to give to every syllable. He had all the parts of an excellent orator.
> (Richard Flecknoe, 1664)

In 1600 language was something to listen to, relish, invent and play with, often very robustly. It has been calculated that, whereas many native English speakers live their lives with a working vocabulary of about 2000 different words, Shakespeare's vocabulary reached over 21,000. Language could become an invigorating assault on the ears and contribute to the sense of a lively, fresh experience which audiences expected at the playhouse.

▶ Listen to (or read a transcript of) a politician's speech in parliament or at a party conference. Pick out examples of rhetoric (formal or/and heightened language). Now reread a few Shakespeare speeches (of ten or more lines) and listen to them for their pattern and repetition. Read them aloud to emphasise these qualities.

Playing with illusion

How can the boards of the playhouse be made to represent Venice, Rome, Athens, a bedchamber, a forest, a tomb, a nunnery – all the evocative places that Shakespeare's stories require? But these were stories to be *presented* rather than places to be *represented*. When Prospero wants to leave his magical island at the end of *The Tempest* he refers to 'this bare island', indicating the empty stage on which the story has been told. As he does so, he acknowledges the audience whose imagination has helped to create the island. He asks them to do him one last service so that he can be released from being Prospero and return to the shadow-player that he has always been.

Specific locations within the story of a play are told through language rather than scenery. 'Well, this is the forest of Arden', says Rosalind when *As You Like It* moves from court to country. Arden is therefore accepted as fact within the illusion of the play, but exactly what she thinks about this new place will be conveyed in her tone of voice and in Touchstone's reply: 'Aye, now am I in Arden, the more fool I!' When the action of *The Winter's Tale* moves from Sicilia to a desolate sea-coast in Act 3, the old nobleman Antigonus is about to abandon the baby Perdita. He is apprehensive about the morality of his task, he is in a strange place and a storm is imminent. Shakespeare quickly establishes place and mood:

> ANTIGONUS Thou art perfect then our ship hath touched upon
> The deserts of Bohemia?
> MARINER   Ay, my lord, and fear
> We have landed in ill time. The skies look grimly
> And threaten present blusters. In my conscience,
> The heavens with that we have in hand are angry
> And frown upon's.

Shakespeare often used powerful language to create storms, which then punctuate the action of the play, often to switch to a new location. Shipwrecks open *Twelfth Night*, *The Tempest* and *The Comedy of Errors*. In *King Lear* a storm takes the action from Gloucester's castle to the heath, and in *Othello* from Venice to Cyprus. A storm is also a shorthand way of announcing general turmoil: it helps an audience to make connections between heavenly anger, political chaos – and even madness within the central character.

Some plays employ a **Chorus**, who acknowledges the fiction of the play and enables the playwright to skip over parts of the story that the audience needs to know but which are difficult to stage. In *Henry V* (Act 3) he speaks especially vivid language:

> Suppose that you have seen
> The well-appointed king at Hampton Pier
> Embark his royalty, and his brave fleet
> With silken streamers the young Phoebus feigning.
> Play with your fancies, and in them behold
> Upon the hempen tackle ship-boys climbing.
> Hear the shrill whistle, which doth order give
> To sounds confused …

Here he openly manipulates the audience's imagination, referring not just to the lively scene but also to the audience as they respond to it. The Chorus in *The Winter's Tale* has a more symbolic value. He tells the audience to skip over sixteen years but also, as Time himself, he influences human affairs. Greene's story, which was the source of the play, was subtitled simply *The Triumph of Time*, but Shakespeare gives Time (Act 4) a more complicated role:

> I that please some, try all, both joy and terror
> Of good and bad, that makes and unfolds error …

Human life is broadly controlled by the passing of time. Within time, the playwright's story occupies stretches of day and night. Plays were presented in full daylight with none of our technical facilities for creating darkness or subtle atmospheric lighting. The actor's words and tone gave the cue and audiences expected to contribute by imagining the fictitious scene. *A Midsummer Night's Dream* is chiefly a night-time story and so depended on the audience making its own adjustments. In Act 3 Hermia gives the instructions:

> Dark night, that from the eye his function takes,
> The ear more quick of apprehension makes;
> Wherein it doth impair the seeing sense
> It pays the hearing double recompense.

Knowing this, the audience can more easily accept the chaos that follows. Oberon tells Puck to 'overcast the night' and to cover 'the starry welkin' with 'drooping fog', so that all four lovers see nothing, spend their energy in ludicrous incompetence and finally collapse in exhaustion. The critic Alan Dessen has summarised the difference between theatre convention then and now: 'For us one figure fails to see another *because* the stage is dark; for them one figure failed to see another and *therefore* the stage was *assumed* to be dark.'

The ways Elizabethan players and audiences regarded stage illusion derives from the travelling players. With the audience around three (or even four) sides of the stage, it was impossible to create convincing illusion or to conceal the conditions of 'playing'. Theatre was a sort of game in which both players and audience accepted the rules or theatre conventions. But it would be wrong to dismiss this as a primitive inadequacy; indeed playing with the effects of illusion could produce great sophistication, as in the layers of gender playing in *As You Like It* (see extract in Part 4, page 95). Shakespeare and other playwrights were also ready to refer to the shared illusion of the play. In *Twelfth Night* Fabian reinforces the remarkable achievement of tricking the pompous steward Malvolio: 'If this were played upon a stage now, I could condemn it as an improbable fiction.' In Act 2 of *As You Like It* Duke Senior plays with the idea that the world is actually a type of theatre:

> This wide and universal theatre
> Presents more woeful pageants than the scene
> Wherein we play in.

Jaques agrees. He goes a step further ('All the world's a stage ...') and suggests that types of unhappiness in life imitate what happens on stage.

Shakespeare often provides layers of illusion by incorporating a play within his play. In the final act of *Love's Labours Lost* and *A Midsummer Night's Dream* struggling amateurs try to entertain the aristocrats, who mock their inadequacy, so providing a moral mirror of behaviour for the real-life audience in the playhouse. In *Hamlet* travelling players visit the castle of Elsinore. Hamlet wants more from them than entertainment. Their fictional play 'The Murder of Gonzago' is to prompt the king into exposing his real-life guilt as a murderer. The theatre audience watches Hamlet and Horatio, who are carefully watching the king watching the players tell their story. The tension within this playing is further heightened because Hamlet is nervously eager that the players perform convincingly. He has just asked them to show discretion, not to strut or bellow, but 'to hold as 'twere the mirror up to nature'. Again Shakespeare has drawn attention to the play as fiction and to the techniques needed to express it.

Part of the audience's pleasure in hearing the play was in recognising that they were sharing an illusion. This is the opposite of what we are often asked to do in the modern theatre or cinema, where we 'suspend our disbelief' in order to enter totally into the life of the fiction as though it were real. Shakespeare's audience expected to respond both within and outside the fiction. Thus at the end of *The Winter's Tale* Shakespeare attempts an unusually bold experiment. Paulina stands before the statue of Hermione and tells the onstage audience: 'It is required / You do awake your faith.' They must believe that a cold stone statue could be made to move like a human being. When they suspend their disbelief and enter into the supposed 'truth' of this illusion, then they realise that Hermione is alive and has been pretending to be the statue of herself. Her 'warm life' has imitated a sculptor's art. And so the 'faith' of Leontes accepting the offered illusion opens the way for the marvellous reunions in the final moments of this play. And outside this onstage audience is the watching theatre audience, who know, even while responding to the emotion of the moment, that all is illusion. But they are happy to pretend to be tricked.

Samuel Johnson, the 18th-century critic, wrote: 'The truth is, that the audience are always in their senses, and know, from the first to the last, that the stage is only a stage, and that the players are only players.'

Playing the woman

In England, though not on the continent, the companies were all male. Women's roles were played by boys and by young men whose voices were unbroken (puberty generally arrived later in Elizabethan times than it does today). There were two types of boy player:

- Those working as trainees with the adult companies, performing in the large outdoor playhouses, and serving an apprenticeship like that in any other profession. They joined at age ten to thirteen and could play female roles until they were twenty. Often they would remain with the company to play male roles and to become financial sharers.

- Children's companies, performing in their own right, often with plays written specially for them. These derived from educational practice in choir schools, but from the 1570s they were managed on a commercial basis. Some children, like the famous Nathan Field, moved across to the adult companies. The boys' early training in music and singing was useful for Shakespeare, especially in plays such as *As You Like It*, *A Midsummer Night's Dream* and *The Tempest*.

Puritan and other moral opponents of theatre were likely to harass the first group more than the second. The adult companies had emerged from the vagabond troupes, whereas the children's companies had a respectable academic pedigree. Their schools considered acting to be valuable 'for the emboldening of the junior scholars, to arm them with audacity'. The stage prepared boys for public life and their performances could be heard as a type of oratory. (In fact, the word 'acting' was associated with the formal actions and gestures of the orator in a 'theatre'. The

more usual word for performing was 'playing' which took place in the 'playhouse'.)
Shakespeare is teasingly prepared to draw attention within his plays to this
convention of boys playing women. In Act 5 of *Antony and Cleopatra*, Cleopatra
describes how she might be humiliated if she were taken as a prisoner to Rome:

> I shall see
> Some squeaking Cleopatra boy my greatness
> I'th'posture of a whore.

She is appalled less by the prospect of being played by a boy (which could be both
convincing and flattering), but by the boy's insolence in mocking her as a whore.
Shakespeare was clearly confident, as were audiences in general, that boys could
personate women in a great variety of moods, and not merely as **caricatures**.

It is not surprising that players were condemned by Puritans and city authorities,
who had a vested interest in traditional good order. Plays were often lively, convincing
and subversive in their subject matter, and could encourage independent thought
– and even lead to protest. Boys playing women could be thought a particular type
of subversion because it confused the accepted distinction between men (who were
supposed to be assertive) and women (who were meant to be placid). Boys trained in
'audacity' found roles that challenged the accepted female role of patient submission.
Shakespeare wrote Lady Macbeth, Beatrice, Portia, Cleopatra and Paulina so that a
spirited boy could express them. A precocious boy's trained wit could remain detached
to challenge and mock, but Shakespeare sometimes put his women in sexually charged
situations too. Hence the complaints about the homoerotic possibilities of boys dressed
as women in male companies and even that they might excite lust in male audiences.

Disguise could complicate the problem of gender. In *Twelfth Night* the boy
actor playing Viola disguises 'herself' as Cesario in order to cope more freely in
a foreign and male world. When Viola feels trapped between Orsino and Olivia,
she laments that she is a 'monster', meaning an unnatural creature: a 'mannish'
woman. But Shakespeare understood the dramatic possibilities of disguise, not
just for the sake of plot, but because a challenging young heroine and a witty page
boy have enough similarities for a precocious boy to play them both convincingly.
At times Shakespeare draws attention to the similarity, as when Orsino tells Viola/
Cesario that her/his feminine appearance may be persuasive with Olivia.

Having boy players also allowed some shrewd doubling. In *King Lear,* Cordelia
and the Fool could be played by the same boy; both challenge and disconcert Lear
but they are sensitive to his welfare in ways that can often seem hidden. They never
appear together on stage, but a link is suggested when a Knight speaks of their
mutual affection: 'Since my young lady's going into France, sir, the fool hath much
pined away.' It has been suggested that in *The Winter's Tale* the same boy could

play both the lost son Mamillius and the found daughter Perdita, so helping to focus the play's theme of brutal error followed by redemption.

As You Like It is Shakespeare's most dazzlingly complicated playing with gender (see extract in Part 4, page 95). Indeed, gender experiment may be seen more as the play's theme than as simply a method of storytelling. At the centre is the boy actor playing the heroine Rosalind who disguises herself as the pageboy Ganymede who then assumes the role of a wayward and volatile Rosalind for a courtship game with the hero Orlando. After all these layers of playing games he/she steps forward to speak the play's Epilogue: Rosalind's 'he' addresses the women in the audience and the 'she' speaks to the men. The play was probably never intended to be a realistic version of men and women in love. Both the play's title and its layers of gender imply that it is more of a fantasy, an 'as you may like it' experiment about different types of love. Boys playing the female roles can supply a degree of detachment that helps the play's rapid switches of role and attitudes.

Clowns

The golden age of Elizabethan theatre grew from mixed origins. From the early 14th to the middle 16th century, travelling players were entertainers, skilled in music, dance and acrobatics. Their most valued members were the clowns who were talented also in **extempore** wit and vulgar jokes. They were both applauded and attacked: ordinary people enjoyed the sense of holiday and often subversive mockery the clowns would provide, but town authorities deplored the ways they could unsettle normal attitudes and routine. 'Playing' was thought to be the opposite of work and associated with idleness; from idleness it can be a short step to disorder.

Players who belonged to companies, including clowns, did not always have a clear-cut status. Companies were often employed by noblemen, and company players sometimes wore their livery as part of the noble household. The relationship could go further. Sir Philip Sidney, the most famous nobleman in the 1580s, was godfather to Richard Tarleton's son. Tarleton was the most talented clown of his day, with astonishing skills in what would now be called stand-up comedy. He worked for The Lord Chamberlain's Men and The Queen's Men until his death in 1588. He was short, squat and robust, specialising in rustic roles, often alongside Robert Wilson, who was a more scholarly wit; their complementary skills gave varied entertainment in double-act performance, just as comedians often work nowadays. As today, crowds would be attracted by their charisma as star performers more than for the plays they performed. Tarleton died before Shakespeare's career had started, but his mixture of skills anticipated the role of Autolycus in *The Winter's Tale*.

The last great Elizabethan clown was Will Kempe, famous more for jigs and dances than for his wit. He worked for The Lord Chamberlain's Men until 1599 and gave the first performance in many of Shakespeare's comedies in the 1590s. But by then the status of players was changing. The permanent playhouses in London had established public drama as more substantial than merely knock-about entertainment, so that players of tragedy like Alleyn and Burbage had replaced clowns as the star performers. Hamlet comments on contemporary acting and clearly feels that extempore clowning can cheapen good writing:

> And let those that play your clowns speak no more than is set down for them, for there be of them that will themselves laugh, to set on some quantity of barren spectators to laugh too, though in the meantime some necessary question of the play be then to be considered.

Playwrights were also influenced by their star performers. Shakespeare wrote major tragic roles with Burbage in mind. He also knew the special qualities of his clowns. When Kempe left the company in 1599, he was replaced by Robert Armin, a more thoughtful and subtle performer. Armin was also a fine singer, and so it was appropriate that soon after his arrival Shakespeare wrote Feste for him in *Twelfth Night*. A few years later he played the Fool in *King Lear*. Both roles require good singing and both have an edgy and melancholic quality. Neither role is very long, but each has always attracted serious actors who can also be skilful clowns.

Although the clown was a specialist role, other actors had to be versatile and move easily between serious and comic playing. Benedick in *Much Ado About Nothing* can be categorised as both hero and clown. Richard Burbage is best remembered for his Hamlet, King Lear and Macbeth, but he also succeeded in Ben Jonson's comedies. Similarly, there was no rigid distinction between types of play. From the 1560s it was common to mix tragic and comic in a single play: Preston's *Cambises* is described on the title page a 'Lamentable Tragedy, Mixed Full of Pleasant Mirth'.

This hybrid form parallels the ambivalent figure of the Vice, commonly found in late medieval Morality plays, to entice people away from the path of virtue. He was a particular type of clown and needed the same performance skills. His behaviour was both terrifying and ludicrous; his role could both amuse and warn. This could produce a complicated unease in the audience response. Shakespeare had learned from this when he created the Witches and the Porter in *Macbeth* and the more substantial character of Richard III. Mixing the serious and comic went further than inventing individual characters. Shakespeare also developed comic subplots for his tragedies: the story of Iago and Roderigo anticipates Iago's trickery of Othello; in *King Lear* Edmund is a type of comic Vice figure when he ill-treats Gloucester, whose story acts as subplot for Lear's.

Stage directions

Shakespeare wrote very few stage directions into his scripts. Apart from entrances and exits, little more was needed, since playwrights were writing for immediate rehearsal when they would probably be on hand to advise the actors. They were not writing these plays to be published. Most of the directions we read today have been added much later by editors, who try to recover either the playwright's intentions or the players' first interpretations – and these may well differ from each other. There are very few accounts of early 17th-century plays in performance. Even those that exist may not be factually accurate: they may describe not what actually appeared on stage, but what an audience imagined as a result of the players' skills.

Some editors try to solve these difficulties by inventing often quite full directions that the words could suggest. Others leave the possibilities open to decisions made in the rehearsal room. At the end of *As You Like It* the boy actor playing Rosalind enters with the actor who plays Hymen, the god of marriage. If 'she' (Rosalind) enters 'as herself' as one modern edition has it, then she will be dressed as a woman. If she is simply left as 'Rosalind', as the directions have named her through the earlier Ganymede scenes, then she could still look like a boy. This will have visual consequences for the final pairing up and for the epilogue.

Much good dramatic writing contains its own implicit stage directions. Consider, for example, a character's movement and manner. In Act 2 of *Romeo and Juliet* Friar Lawrence sees Juliet coming towards his cell:

> Here comes the lady. O, so light a foot
> Will ne'er wear out the everlasting flint.

In Act 3 Juliet, excited and happy, sees her Nurse enter, but Shakespeare gives four lines more of Juliet's energy before they speak together. This gap covers the Nurse's slow shuffling across the stage. She has depressing news and her speech conveys an agitated hopelessness:

> Ah, weraday, he's dead, he's dead, he's dead!
> We are undone, lady, we are undone.

In Act 2 of *Macbeth*, it is dark night, the guests are in bed and the stillness compels Macbeth into a horrified sense of the evil around him. He identifies himself with a personification of murder, which moves towards the king's bedchamber:

> and withered murder,
> Alarumed by his sentinel, the wolf,
> Whose howl's his watch, thus with his stealthy pace,
> With Tarquin's ravishing strides, towards his design
> Moves like a ghost.

These lines include direct references to movement: 'stealthy', 'like a ghost'. Macbeth seems to move with it – 'thus' – and the actor would instinctively feel the rhythm of the writing: its extended wariness; its sense of forbidden fascination through the sexually charged story of Prince Tarquin about to rape Lucrece; finally, the little rhythmic kick of extra pace in 'Moves like a ghost'.

The texts, as we read them today, are divided into acts and scenes, as though Shakespeare were writing five-act plays in the style of classical Greek drama. These divisions first appeared in the 1623 Folio edition and were added to help readers of his plays, not actors in staging them. When proscenium theatres developed after 1660, these breaks in the action were used for scenic effects and elaborate visual changes (see Part 2, page 46). This practice is not the fashion today – nor was it when Shakespeare was writing, though his later plays, often performed at the indoor Blackfriars Theatre, needed some pauses for trimming the candles that provided the artificial light. In general, Shakespeare wrote his plays for continuous action on stage.

An interesting example occurs early in *Much Ado About Nothing*. The villain Don John and his two followers are conspiring, presumably **downstage**, to wreck Claudio's marriage to Hero. Then they leave and 'Act 1 ends'. But the action continues with Leonato's entry and first words of Act 2: 'Was not Count John here at supper?' His question is not prompted by offstage discussion with his family, but because he sees Don John sneaking away through another door. This link ensures fluent playing of the action from group to group. It also heightens the drama of misunderstanding, as Beatrice jokes briefly about Don John's gloom: the malcontent is dismissed as merely a boring outsider and his potential danger overlooked.

Sometimes the contrast between scenes brings ironic focus to the drama, as in Act 5 of *Hamlet*. Horatio has been trying to persuade Hamlet to withdraw from the duel with Laertes, but Hamlet prefers to submit to whatever Fate has in store for him. Neither Hamlet nor Horatio knows what villainy the king has been preparing under cover of an honourable contest of swordsmanship. The two friends talk quietly, surrounded by the vast space of the otherwise empty stage. Suddenly the doors open and ceremonial music brings on the king and the court, with all its movement and colour. They descend upon Hamlet with what appears to be gracious welcome. To an audience Hamlet will still seem alone (and vulnerable) in the centre of this crowd, even though the play's tempo has greatly altered.

Since drama dramatises conflict, and sometimes confrontation, it is often effective when this is reinforced by a formal symmetry. Shakespeare's writing invites this in Act 1 Scene 1 of *Romeo and Juliet* when the two families are censured by the Duke, and even more at the end of the play when both Montague and Capulet have to face the results of their hostility. The Duke requires the two fathers to step forward. Now they compete in their penitence and each promises to erect a statue in tribute to the lovers. The situation and the language at this moment are generally matched in performance by formal grouping on stage.

The unpredictable violence in *Richard III* is eventually formalised into a battle of good versus evil, Richmond against Richard. Both leaders erect their tents on the battlefield, and each is visited at night by the ghosts of Richard's victims: in an eerie ritual each ghost promises support for one and disaster for the other. Each leader wakes in the morning, Richmond with health and vigour, Richard exhausted and neurotic; then each makes his speech to his troops. This series of events, with matching language and symmetrical staging, tells the audience that, though living with violence is chaotic, above it all an organising destiny presides over contrasting fortunes. *Richard III* brings to an end a hundred years of conflict which Shakespeare has dramatised in his eight Chronicle Plays. The horror and tumult of this complicated story are now resolved in formal stagecraft.

▶ Focus on any play by Shakespeare that you know well and list moments where you feel stage directions for the actors are implied in the writing. Try to make your list as varied as possible.

Soliloquy

A soliloquy (literally, speaking alone) is a dramatic convention. It was particularly effective on the Elizabethan public stage, which jutted out into the centre of the playhouse and was surrounded by audience. Soliloquy works in two ways at the same time:

- The player is alone and addresses the audience.

- The character he plays believes himself to be alone. He explores his own thoughts, often engaging in internal debate, while the audience overhears.

Soliloquy gave Shakespeare several opportunities:

- It provided extremely close contact between player and audience so that feelings, ideas and plans could be shared. In Act 2 of *King Lear* two of the more admirable characters, both suffering, are given adjacent soliloquies: Kent, in the stocks, reflects on his master's plight and reads Cordelia's letter; Edgar, hunted as a criminal, tells the audience about his plans to impersonate a lunatic.

- Sometimes the audience could enjoy having superior knowledge, as in *Twelfth Night* when the pompous steward Malvolio gives Viola the ring, believing and claiming that Viola/Cesario had earlier given it to Olivia. The audience appreciates the mistake, then enjoys seeing Viola suddenly realise: 'I left no ring with her: what means this lady? / Fortune forbid my outside have not charmed her!'

- Soliloquy allowed a clown to play to the audience as stand-up comics do nowadays. In *Othello* Iago plays the clown and his soliloquies bring him downstage. Othello, the more serious role, is generally placed at a more dignified distance from the audience. This is one reason why the more mobile Iago so often upstages Othello – or was it downstaged in the Elizabethan theatre? In *Much Ado About Nothing* Benedick is both leading man and clown. When, in Act 2, his friends trick him into thinking that Beatrice loves him, he shares his thought-processes with the audience and provokes them into amused reactions:

  > Shall quips and sentences, and these paper bullets of the brain awe a man from the career of his humour? No, the world must be peopled. When I said I would die a bachelor, I did not think I should live till I were married.

- There could be teasing moral complications when a villain assumes complicity with an audience, describing plans and sharing delight when they succeed. Edmund and Iago both use soliloquy in this way. Sometimes the complicity is sharpened by challenges that seem to invite the audience into active participation. In Act 1 of Shakespeare's early play *Richard III* the deformed hero scores an unlikely success when he woos Lady Anne, and then turns to the audience with questions:

  > Was ever woman in this humour wooed?
  > Was ever woman in this humour won?

An audience can enjoy his success and also deplore his ruthlessness.

- Soliloquy brought dramatic variety into the storytelling. If a scene with several players has occupied the upstage area, the stage is suddenly cleared apart from the one isolated character, who advances downstage to speak with the audience. In a theatre like The Globe he would occupy the front edge of the platform, the central point of the playhouse.

- The soliloquy could be a private climax to a scene, especially if a large public scene has just finished. For example, the first court scene in *Hamlet* shows the hero dressed in black, making a conspicuous protest against the upbeat public relations of King Claudius' court, but he says very little. The audience has to wait until line 129 before hearing his disgust with his mother/queen and uncle/king. This soliloquy also provides dramatic punctuation between the high status of the court (which ought to be Prince Hamlet's milieu) and the lower status of ordinary people, with whom he feels more at ease.

In Shakespeare's time the player would probably address his soliloquy directly to the audience, rather than speak within himself, allowing them to overhear his thoughts. When theatre design changed after 1660 and plays were performed within the picture frame of the proscenium arch, this convention of playing to the audience could seem odd. The arrival of film and television has led to other ways of dealing with soliloquy, such as the 'voice-over'. Nowadays, directors and actors, using a variety of theatre spaces, will feel free to make many different decisions about how to deliver a soliloquy.

▶ Practise speaking (part of) one of Shakespeare's soliloquies:
(a) in robust style, as for a large theatre
(b) more intimately, as for a small studio theatre
(c) as for The Globe Theatre.
What were the differences you felt you had to make?

▶ Learn the passage by heart. Notice how much greater freedom of interpretation you have when speaking the lines from memory than when reading from the page.

Costume

In *Hamlet* Act 1 Scene 3 the young man Laertes is about to leave for the fashion-conscious city of Paris. His father, Polonius, wants him to make a good impression, and, among other instructions, he reminds him that 'the apparel oft proclaims the man'. Shakespeare's plays are full of kings, dukes, cardinals, fine ladies and extravagant young men. Status and vitality had to be expressed in colour and style, to match the gaudy painting of the theatre itself. The plays also included lawyers, doctors, soldiers and uniformed servants. Companies had a huge turnover of different plays, many with long lists of characters. It follows that they needed a large stock of costumes, or 'apparel', as the Elizabethans called it. This amounted to an expensive investment, since the materials, such as velvet, satin, silk, damask, were authentic. Many were cast-offs bought from noble households. In 1599 a Swiss visitor, Thomas Platter, commented:

> The comedians are most expensively and elegantly apparelled. It is the English usage for eminent lords or knights at their decease to bequeath and leave almost the best of their clothes to their serving men, which it is unseemly for the latter to wear, so they offer them for sale for the actors to purchase.

There were also special scenes in Shakespeare's comedies and romances where gods and masque-like characters would intervene to influence human affairs: the fairy world in *A Midsummer Night's Dream*, for instance; Hymen at the end of

As You Like It; or Ariel's spectacular transformations in *The Tempest*. Some of these costumes required particular designs to convey allegorical meaning. *Henry IV Part 2* opens with the unsettling figure of Rumour; he wore a robe 'painted full of tongues'. These moments, designed for astonishment, would have to outclass the other scenes in the impact of their costume. No wonder Henslowe, the manager of The Lord Admiral's Men, fined players very heavily if they left the theatre wearing company costumes.

Though costume was often lavish, there was little interest in period accuracy. A famous drawing of *Titus Andronicus* in performance shows a mixture of Elizabethan doublets and Roman togas. Costume had immediate effect: broadly to impress audiences, and in greater detail to indicate attitudes. This could be especially important for battles: in *Antony and Cleopatra* the tough Romans against the exotic Egyptians; in *Henry V* the 'war-worn coats' of the depleted English facing the over-confident style and colour of the French. In the latter play dress has an effect when understated: it signifies genuine, dignified purpose when the king, disguising his status, borrows Sir Thomas Erpingham's humble cloak. In *The Merchant of Venice* the showy Christians oppose the Jewish outsiders. They co-exist uneasily in the same city, with its reputation for conspicuous fashion. But Shylock in his simple 'gabardine' lives an austere life following his religious beliefs. He warns his daughter against the self-indulgent Christians with their masks ('varnished faces') as they prepare for their carnival. Which group would audiences support? Costume contributes to the complex moral judgements.

King Lear's costume clearly shows his status. At first when he presides formally over his court, his dress would display authority. In Act 3 he goes mad and strips off his 'lendings', his kingly trappings, which he now discovers are no part of the essential human being; he sees himself as 'unaccommodated man', who is alarmingly close to the animals. In Act 4 he is released from his suffering and cherished by his daughter Cordelia; he wakes from the past to find himself in simple, fresh garments, which signify redemption.

But at court, theatre could become far more lavish, especially in the masques (see page 10, above) created for James I. There the architect, Inigo Jones, spent colossal sums on creating coherent design of stage sets and costumes when collaborating with Ben Jonson on their allegorical masques. Jones aimed not to create detailed naturalism but to astonish with colour and invention. These productions, to glorify the mystique of monarchy and to support relations with visiting nobility, were far removed from the conditions of the public theatre.

Battles

Many plays of the period were about politics, history and military events. These often included battles, which invited crowd-pleasing processions, marching, violence, spectacle and skilful swordplay. Staging them would seem difficult for today's audiences, used to cinema effects, but in Shakespeare's time the companies couldn't afford enough players to fill the space, the range of off-stage sound effects was limited and there were no lighting effects to create a believable atmosphere. In *Henry V* Shakespeare tackled the story of the most famous English military success, the Battle of Agincourt, when the king's small army scored an improbable victory over the confident French. How could this be staged convincingly? The Chorus appears to confess Shakespeare's problem to the audience:

> And so our scene must to the battle fly,
> Where (O for pity!) we shall much disgrace,
> With four or five most vile and ragged foils
> Right ill disposed in brawl ridiculous,
> The name of Agincourt. Yet sit and see,
> Minding true things by what their mockeries be.

This is a disingenuous pretence. When he wrote the play in 1599, Shakespeare was a confident and resourceful professional. He asks the audience to use their imagination generously, but does not really believe that he and the players were inadequate. Earlier in this Act 4 speech he has already described the battlefield in brilliantly evocative language: the tense and eerie noises of the night, metallic preparation; clocks that 'toll'; ghostly moonlight – and then a focus on the resilient and cheerful king. The battle itself is shrewdly created by focus on individuals, preparing, encouraging, suffering or stumbling on stage exhausted. The audience was invited to imagine the main violence offstage, supported by drums, trumpets and raucous sounds. On stage two or three soldiers might burst in to suggest triumph, defeat or fighting in single combat with each other. The technique was similar to TV historical documentaries nowadays, in which vivid close-ups on very few soldiers can be made to suggest a larger scene. In the first speech of *Henry V* the Chorus urged the audience:

> Into a thousand parts divide one man,
> And make imaginary puissance. [*puissance*: military power, an army]

In *King Lear* Shakespeare uses an even more effective shorthand. Cordelia's army crosses the stage, followed by the blinded Gloucester. His son Edgar leads him on and leaves. Five lines later Edgar returns with the news that 'King Lear hath lost, he and his daughter ta'en'. Those five lines offered the audience a strange contrast of visual and aural effects: they heard the offstage music, clashes and shouts that denote a battle, but they saw the solitary, shrunken Gloucester surrounded by the vast space of the stage around him. A physical event for crowds has been re-expressed as a nightmare mental state for a single victim.

In a political sense too, battles are significant not for their violent effects but because they decide the fates of great men and nations: Henry VI battered to and fro in the Wars of the Roses; Brutus and Antony confronting each other in *Julius Caesar*; Antony turning tail at the Battle of Actium in *Antony and Cleopatra*. J.L. Styan, in his book *Shakespeare's Stagecraft*, is very persuasive in showing how the rhythm and variety of the short battle scenes present Antony's predicament as it might be achieved in the modern cinema.

From stage to page

Modern directors expect to work from page to stage: they start with a book containing the text of a printed play, and then interpret and rehearse it for per-formance. However, Shakespeare's plays began their life through his collaboration with the company of players. The purpose of a play was that it should be seen and heard; reading it later in quarto or folio form – books of different sizes – was a different (and lesser) activity.

The script belonged to the company so that if and when it was printed, the printed editions usually specified the company's name. Generally the playwright's status was incidental – like that of the writer, or committee of writers, for big screenplays in today's film industry. Shakespeare's love poem *Venus and Adonis*, published in 1593, gave him far more status for eloquence than his plays. It was reprinted six times during his lifetime.

Though Shakespeare's plays were constantly performed, they were not collected together until the First Folio of 1623, seven years after his death. So it is helpful to consider most of their progress in a direction unfamiliar to us: from stage to page. Generally the processes ran like this:

1 From playwright to stage

- The playwright would be paid for the script and then the company would hold the rights.

- The script (the working drafts of the play were known as 'foul papers') was copied twice, into two 'fair papers'.

- One copy was cut up into parts, one for each of the players (brief cues were added).

- The other fair copy was sent to the Master of the Revels, a court official, who would indicate any objections (e.g. blasphemy, subversive comments) and changes required, and who would then issue a licence for its performance.

- On its return to the company, the book-keeper would amend the script as required and add some basic stage directions.

- This final version of the script became the 'prompt book', the basis for performance.

2 From stage to the printed book

- Sometimes playwrights, defying the company's rights, might sell their play in quarto form. (A quarto is a sheet of paper, folded in half twice, giving four leaves or eight pages.)

- Sometimes even more unauthorised versions would appear, the script gathered by a writer's observation, memory and from actors. These 'pirated' copies were generally very inaccurate.

- In 1623 Heminge and Condell, professionals with Shakespeare in The King's Men, published the First Folio of his plays. They wanted to celebrate their friend's work and also to counter the various imperfect quartos and other versions that existed. (A folio is a sheet that has been folded in half to make two pages or four leaves. It is larger than a quarto and can make a distinguished, expensive and elegant volume.)

Collaboration between different playwrights and between playwright and players was a lively and enriching process, but makes it difficult to establish the 'purity' of a written text. Shakespeare supplied a script but expected his friends and colleagues to add much that was needed for its performance. He would often indicate an actor's entry but not his exit; sometimes a song is included but not the name of the character who sings it. Perhaps he would expect to supply this sort of information orally. He was probably also happy for his colleagues to fill in the gaps as part of their collaborative working experience. He would not have expected the precise detailed analysis that critics give to his writing nowadays, nor the complicated tasks that he set for future editors as they try to establish the definitive, authentic text.

The First Folio

The First Folio is crucial for understanding the Shakespeare we know, read and perform today. In Shakespeare's time it was unusual to produce a book of plays. Ben Jonson did it in 1616, but he was quarrelsome and very sensitive about his status as an artist. Being a prolific playwright, he intended to raise the status of play-writing to that of history, theology, classical texts and poetry, all of which gained dignity from appearing in print. Writing plays was considered a lower-grade activity, rather like casual journalism today. Shakespeare (and possibly even the self-important Jonson) would have been astonished by the literary status given to their plays today.

The First Folio contains 36 plays, 18 of which had not appeared previously in quarto form. Heminge and Condell took care to consult 'prompt books' from the first playhouse performances. They were struggling against years of confusion: since Shakespeare's first draft every play had been subject to deliberate revision, to accidental alteration in performance, and to the effects of pirated versions. The 2007 Folio edition for the Royal Shakespeare Company has aimed to convey the level of authenticity achieved in 1623. Its editor Jonathan Bate, also trying to remove even more years of confusion, challenges the practice of merging Quarto and Folio editions of the plays that began with the growth of Shakespeare scholarship in the early 18th century.

A famous case of merging two versions was Nicholas Rowe's composite *Hamlet*. He found a soliloquy in the Quarto that does not appear in the Folio. In Act 4 Hamlet laments 'How all occasions do inform against me' so that he continues to delay in his 'duty' of revenge. This has lent weight to the idea that Hamlet is paralysed by self-questioning, or, as Laurence Olivier put it in his famous film 'the man who could not make up his mind'. But the Folio Hamlet is much more decisive once the Players' performance has convinced him of the King's guilt.

▶ Take about 50 lines of any Shakespeare play you don't know well. Give each actor a copy of just his/her own part, plus a one-line cue for each speech. Rehearse the scene using these scripts, and then discuss what you have discovered from this unusual process.

Players under attack

Just as plays often dealt with awkward and dangerous topics, so the players found their profession itself criticised and challenged. The more popular they were with audiences, the more they alarmed the city authorities and religious reformers.

There were several reasons why players came under attack from the authorities:

- Health: in summer outbreaks of plague were common, and infection spread rapidly when crowds, such as theatre audiences, were gathered.

- Safety: as with football today, playhouse crowds could be volatile, and riots become more likely.

- Time-wasting: plays caused apprentices to waste their master's time and money when they were lured to playhouses during the working day.

- Crime: playhouses drew large audiences to sleazy areas of the city, an obvious hunting ground for pickpockets and prostitutes.

- Church attendance: this was weakened when plays were performed at the same time as church services.

- Sedition: plays often promoted seditious opinions that could encourage rebellion and threaten state (and church) authority. These opinions on stage could be far more potent for a semi-literate population than when read in pamphlets.

- Promoting immoral behaviour: some Puritan sects opposed frivolous entertainment, believing it to undermine a sober regard for godly values. Cross-dressing (boys playing women) was often attacked for encouraging sexual deviation (see page 29, above).

- Dangerous vanities: playhouses were gaudy and lively places, like funfairs. They led to enthusiasm for dangerous vanities.

- Hypocrisy: drama is based on pretending, thus to some people, especially religious reformers, it is based on lying and deception. (The word 'hypocrite' originally meant 'actor' in Greek.) 'We are commanded by God to abide in the same calling wherein we were called', wrote Stephen Gosson (a Puritan and satirist). He believed that a young man dressing up, swaggering on a stage, pretending to be a prince, was irreligious hypocrisy.

Naturally players defended themselves. They pointed out that many plays defend good order and support the authorities; that tragedy shows how wicked conduct is punished by suffering and death; that plays often expose corruption in church and state.

Throughout history the question of censorship has troubled society at large. The arts generally, and especially the performing arts, require free creativity and free speech, to explore often painful and controversial areas of human life. Therefore writers for theatre, cinema and TV may find themselves on the fringes of what public opinion finds acceptable. And the difficulties are further complicated by the fact that fashions change in censuring and censoring material that concerns politics, sex and violence. (All of Shakespeare's plays explore one or more of these three aspects of human life). For example, the limits of what was acceptable in 1600 differ from the standards of Thomas Bowdler in 1818 (see page 51) and from audiences in 1950 and again in the 21st century.

2 | Shakespeare in performance after 1660

- How far has taste determined the ways in which Shakespeare is performed?

- Who has most influence on a production: actors, director, audience or critics?

- In what ways have different styles of theatre shaped different ways of playing Shakespeare?

- What is meant by the 'afterlife' of a Shakespeare play?

Late 17th century: Shakespeare 'improved'

In 1660 Charles II came to the throne, 11 years after the execution of his father Charles I. The period of Puritan restriction on theatres was over and the term '**Restoration**' was used to describe the revival of the monarchy. It was also used to describe the drama and literature which flourished in these more welcoming times.

During the Restoration, Shakespeare was respected and performed but had no special status. Critics of the time praised Shakespeare for his creative instincts, but regretted that he had lived in a less refined age that often ignored classical Greek ideals. ''Twas a fine garden,' wrote the critic Flecknoe, 'but it wanted weeding.' They found their contemporary models in France, which produced the **neo-classical** plays of Molière in comedy and Racine in tragedy. French tastes and fashion greatly influenced elegant London life in the late 17th century: in food, clothes and manners, as well as literature and art.

There were several aspects of Shakespeare's writing that caused concern to critics:

- His language was often unrefined ('barbarous') in its puns and gross humour. Restoration writers and critics prized elegance in thought and language.

- Though his characters were 'natural', their language was too loaded with metaphor.

- He lacked 'Art', the refined understanding and technique that neo-classical critics expected authors to imitate from the classical Greek texts. For example:
  - his plots sprawled and contained too many incidental characters
  - he failed to observe the classical unities of time and place
  - his tragedies were not written wholly in elevated heroic verse; they also contained elements of comedy, farce and prose writing
  - some of the violence in his plays occurred onstage instead of being reported.

- He often ignored 'poetic justice', which requires good characters to flourish at the end and the wicked to be punished. For this 'failure' he was criticised for offering no clear moral direction.

The critics' remedy was to 'improve' Shakespeare, with adaptation and rewriting that went far beyond previous reworkings. These adaptations were also influenced by changed conditions in the theatre. In general, audiences were more courtly and fashionable than those of Shakespeare's time. Actresses now played the female roles – and in some cases they played young men in what were called 'breeches' roles, which anticipated the more recent tradition of a 'principal boy' played by a young woman in pantomimes. The large public playhouses for which Shakespeare wrote were replaced by smaller indoor theatres, often well equipped with movable scenery and machines for special effects. Actresses and improved spectacle were popular with audiences; to include them made Shakespeare's plays more marketable. Here are some examples of the ways in which Shakespeare's plays were 'improved':

- In 1679 the playwright Thomas Otway placed the story of Romeo and Juliet against a complicated background of Roman politics, matching the political concerns of Charles II's reign: the threat of Catholic plots and anxieties about the succession to the throne. Otway's Juliet wakes just after Romeo has drunk the poison, so that the lovers have an anguished scene of farewell. This altered ending continued to be performed through much of the 18th century.

- In Shakespeare's *Macbeth* a sense of evil predominates. If the play was to offer moral instruction, it was felt that some compensating goodness must be included. Therefore when the playwright Sir William Davenant (a staunch supporter of Charles II) revised *Macbeth*, he brought Banquo's son Fleance home from exile in France in time for the final battle. Lady Macduff's role was enlarged, so that she embodied all the feminine domestic virtues that Lady Macbeth lacks. She even warned her husband against the dangers of ambition. Thus what had been a very male play was able to offer more opportunity for actresses – and to please male audiences who liked to see women on the stage.

- The playwright Nahum Tate staged a new version of *King Lear* in 1681. He felt that Shakespeare's ending was too bleak and unjust. His Cordelia endures an attempted rape by Edmund; at the end she survives to marry Edgar and to rule the kingdom with him, while Lear regains his sanity and joins the surviving Gloucester in retirement 'in calm reflections on our fortunes past'. Tate removed the Fool on the grounds that he was too eccentric to appear in a serious tragedy. Tate's *King Lear* continued to be performed regularly until 1838 because it satisfied the popular demand for moral reassurance.

▶ Compare the moral reflections of Edgar, Kent and Albany that end Shakespeare's version of *Lear* with these words spoken by Edgar in Tate's version:

> Divine Cordelia, all the gods can witness
> How much thy love to empire I prefer!
> Thy bright example shall convince the world
> (Whatever storms of fortune are decreed)
> That truth and virtue shall at last succeed.

- In 1667 Davenant combined with the poet John Dryden to rewrite and stage *The Tempest*. They gave Miranda a sister and companions for Ariel and Caliban. Their Prospero, in secret, looks after a male ward who has never seen a woman (just as Miranda is ignorant of men). Later Thomas Shadwell increased the play's song and dance elements so that it became virtually an opera with, for example, classical gods and goddesses in a 'chariot drawn with sea-horses'. The storm, however, remained a spectacular challenge whenever the play was staged.

It was also important for Shakespeare to be politically correct for Restoration times. In his prologue to *The Tempest* Dryden saw Shakespeare as anticipating the revived Stuart dynasty of Charles II:

> As when a tree's cut down the secret root
> Lives underground, and thence new branches shoot;
> So, from old Shakespeare's honour'd dust, this day
> Springs up and buds a new reviving Play.

In this way adapters felt like responsible gardeners, tending old Shakespearean stock by pruning it and making it fit for a more enlightened generation.

▶ Consider the Shakespeare plays that you know and see if you can 'improve' them by tightening the plot and removing some of the incidental characters.

▶ Consider any of Shakespeare's plays that end with good characters suffering and the wicked prospering. Could these plays be improved by more poetic justice?

18th century: Shakespeare and human nature

By the middle of the 18th century, attitudes towards Shakespeare had changed. He came to be seen as a genius, a sort of national icon. He represented 'honest' English virtues against foreign shallowness and deceit. (At this time Protestant England had political difficulties with Catholic France and Spain.)

In 1769 David Garrick, the greatest actor of the age, presided over the Jubilee celebrations (commemorating the 150th anniversary of Shakespeare's death) at Stratford to proclaim the specially English qualities of Shakespeare that made him unique in world drama:

> Our Shakespeare compared is to no man,
> No Frenchman nor Grecian nor Roman.
> Their swans are all geese to the Avon's sweet swan
> And the man of all men was a Warwickshire man.

The 18th-century taste for the sentimental also led to a growing interest in Shakespeare's love stories and domestic scenes rather than heroic grandeur. Tragedies were now not so much awe-inspiring: instead they encouraged audiences to feel pathos and shed tears. This change coincided with the growth of the novel, its domestic stories and romantic heroines in distress. Novels by Richardson, Fielding and Sterne also led to a huge increase in female readers.

In the late 1730s The Shakespeare Ladies Club was formed. For them Shakespeare was the manly genius, suspicious of foreigners and morally far superior to late 17th-century Restoration comedy, infected as it seemed to be with French-inspired sexual promiscuity (though Shakespeare had to be edited to allow this contrast to ring true).

Johnson on Shakespeare

In 1765, the critic Dr Johnson, a powerful arbiter of taste, wrote his *Preface to Shakespeare*. He still objected to what he saw as moral failings: 'He sacrifices virtue to convenience and is so much more careful to please than to instruct that he seems to write without any moral purpose.' Johnson saw Shakespeare less as a playwright and more as a great poet, whose duty was to improve the world into nobler thinking. But Johnson did not insist on formal classical rules. He criticised 'the players', Heminge and Condell, for their arbitrary categories of comedies, histories and tragedies in the 1623 Folio:

> Shakespeare's plays are not in the rigorous and critical sense either tragedies or comedies, but compositions of a distinct kind; exhibiting the real state of sublunary [earth-bound, therefore human] nature, which partakes of good and evil, joy and sorrow.

For Johnson, Shakespeare was 'the poet of nature', who bypassed the neo-classical decorums of art. Even the poet Dryden at the end of the 17th century had defended Shakespeare's lack of formal art, declaring that 'he needed not the spectacles of Books to read Nature'.

Johnson explored Shakespeare's genius in greater detail. He welcomed the contradictory mixtures of real life, in which 'at the same time, the reveller is hasting to his wine, and the mourner burying his friend'. Therefore tragedies may include gross and vulgar elements: Iago bawls vulgarity at Brabantio's window in the opening scene of *Othello*; in *Hamlet* Claudius is a drunkard as well as a king, and Shakespeare can introduce gravediggers to pun and joke while Hamlet prepares for death.

Interpretations of Shakespeare: David Garrick

One of Dr Johnson's close friends was the greatest actor of the century, David Garrick, whose London career began with his *Richard III* in 1741. He was praised for a new and natural style of playing tragedy, unlike the heroic posturing of an earlier generation, though modern audiences would probably still find his style artificial. Garrick aimed to find the inward character of his role and to express it through extreme mobility of face, gesture and body. He was a small, nimble actor with tremendous stage charisma. He was able to switch rapidly from emotion to emotion and could affect an audience by the realism of a slight detail. When, in *King Lear*, the old king is reunited with Cordelia, Garrick, speaking the line 'Be these tears wet?', touched Cordelia's cheek, then held his fingers to the light to see if they glistened. He would observe real life and bring its detail to his performances. He described seeing a father, playing with his daughter at an upper window, accidentally drop the child, who fell to her death. Garrick used the father's grief to influence his Lear, but this was not wholly to interpret Shakespeare's lines better. His priority was to move or excite an audience with a new theatricality.

Garrick aimed to rescue and perform more of what Shakespeare actually wrote from the extremely free adaptations of his work. In this he was helped by numerous editors who tried to establish the authentic texts, though some, like Alexander Pope, tried to detach Shakespeare the poet from the crudeness (as he saw it) of the popular stage. However, Garrick was subject to the popular taste of his day that disliked innovation: his version of *Romeo and Juliet* removed all mention of Romeo loving Rosaline before he met Juliet, and Romeo died in the same manner as in Otway's 1679 version, not Shakespeare's. Garrick was famous for his Hamlet, Richard III and Lear; but, unlike the practice of long runs today, he never played the same role more than 200 times in a 30-year period. Plays would be revived for a few performances and new actors were inducted into the traditional speeches, moves and stage 'business'. Audiences flocked to see Garrick in the great roles (and the play as a secondary attraction) as they do for famous opera singers today.

The theatres

The general conservatism of 18th-century theatre was encouraged by the fact that playhouse design barely changed. The variety of Elizabethan theatre spaces was not repeated after the Restoration; in fact, during Garrick's career (roughly 1740–1780) there was virtually no new theatre building in London. But the theatres were intimate – often cramped, uncomfortable and rowdy. There are many records of audiences barracking, of actors stepping out of role and appealing for co-operation. New plays, and old ones too, were often supplied with prologue speeches for the star actor to deliver, so continuing the old tradition of a company presenting a play, rather than individuals inhabiting their roles as a 20th-century **method actor** would.

▶ Follow an 18th-century practice and try writing a prologue (in rhyming verse if you can) that introduces a Shakespeare play to the audience.

The interior space of the theatre was divided into three basic parts:

- *the audience* in the pit, stalls and galleries (with the noisiest in the cheapest top level)

- *the platform,* lined at the sides with entrances for the actors and boxes for the fashionable audience members

- *the scene* behind the performers, with 'flown' and sliding scenery and facilities for stage effects.

Costume design was random and rudimentary by today's standards. Generally, the leading players would take the finest costumes from the theatre's stock, especially if (as was usual) they were playing grand or fashionable roles. There was rarely any interest in historical accuracy, except occasional gestures towards Roman togas and drapes where the play invited it. In general, costume style was contemporary, with some awareness of French fashions for elegant, foppish caricatures and Spanish for eccentric flamboyance.

Reading the plays

In the late 17th century Shakespeare's plays had been available for reading only in large forbidding folio editions. As editors of Shakespeare competed with each other in the early 18th century, his plays became available separately in small pocket-size editions. This movement both reflected and created a great interest in reading the plays. But though this helped to market Shakespeare on stage, there was a downside to such popularity: Shakespeare was becoming known as 'The Bard', a term that has lasted into modern times. 'Bard' suggests an ancient, venerated poet with prophetic wisdom, fiercely aligned with long-held national values. This invented figure is very different from a lively, practical, flexible playwright who can make his impact on a stage. But the 'Bard' and bardolatry were to guide the **Romantics**' reading of Shakespeare at the end of the 18th century.

1790–1830: towards Romantic revolution

By 1790 Shakespeare had become the unrivalled national playwright and the poet of (human) nature. The 1790s also saw the French Revolution and England's wars with France that continued until the Battle of Waterloo in 1815. In some ways the period was similar to Shakespeare's own lifetime two hundred years earlier: war, threats of war, poor harvests, political unrest, suspicion of foreign spies and English collaborators. The Romantic poets were radical, at times revolutionary, in their thinking: the great poet Wordsworth supported the French Revolution; he and Coleridge were under surveillance for possible treason; Shelley was an atheist and political anarchist; the notorious Lord Byron scandalised and mocked London society and fought for freedom against all types of tyranny. All these anti-establishment Romantic poets worshipped the genius of Shakespeare. Was Shakespeare therefore a questioning dissident or the conservative spokesman for the political status quo? The authorities tried to appropriate him as a conservative. But it was the poets who wrote eloquently about his independent spirit and the actors who staged his plays.

There were, however, restrictions on staging the plays. Until 1843 only three London companies were allowed to perform Shakespeare. This restriction was imposed to keep the Shakespeare heritage pure. Nonetheless, wild rewritings and travesties continued to be staged, such as the 1828 *Hamlet, Prince of Denmark*, in which Hamlet is put on trial for murdering his father, but the queen's confession saves him and eventually he becomes king. It is not surprising that such performances disappointed the Shakespearean purists. The essayist Charles Lamb wrote in 1811 that *King Lear* is diminished by the stage because what the audiences see is bound to be inferior to what the play's sublime poetry makes the reader imagine. In the theatre we see 'only what is painful and disgusting … an old man tottering about the stage with a walking stick'. However, 'while we read it we see not Lear but we are Lear, – we are in his mind, we are sustained by a grandeur which baffles the malice of daughters and storms'.

▶ With reference to the plays you know, debate the issue that Shakespeare's plays show more of their qualities when read on the page than when performed on the stage.

Tragedies such as *King Lear* are always about exceptional individuals who suffer great misfortune and express intense feelings. Actors who are themselves passionate outsiders will have a special affinity for the great roles, particularly in this period of Romantic sensibility. And most of the theatre reviewers in these years were more interested in the characters of Hamlet, Macbeth, Lear, Othello, Shylock, Richard III than in the heroes of Shakespeare's comedies.

Interpretations of Shakespeare: Kemble and Kean

Drury Lane was one of the three theatres licensed to present Shakespeare. Like Garrick (presided 1747–1766) and Henry Irving (presided 1878–1902) at The Lyceum, John Philip Kemble commanded Drury Lane, and then Covent Garden, from 1788 to 1817. He shared many of Shakespeare's plays with the tragedy actress Sarah Siddons. Kemble's beliefs and grave manner supported the establishment, not the revolutionaries. In 1796 his *Henry V* was subtitled 'The Conquest of the French'. His theatres were larger and more grand than Garrick's, he achieved awe-inspiring spectacle and scenic effects, and he employed antiquarian scholars for period accuracy in costume and sets. This started a trend that lasted throughout the 19th century.

Kemble continued to alter Shakespeare's texts and, as we would think, his intentions. For example, he attempted to clean up *Measure for Measure*. This has always been a difficult play, for the following reasons:

- It doesn't fit comfortably into the categories of either comedy or tragedy.

- It appears to undermine authority, in the characters and behaviour of the Duke and Angelo.

- It is difficult for an audience to warm to the heroine, Isabella.

- The ending is complicated by Isabella's silence when the Duke offers marriage (see extract in Part 4, page 98).

- The low-life scenes are about the sex trade in Vienna and are full of bawdy language.

Kemble's version, however, celebrated the wisdom of a benign paternalist ruler, who evidently could have had little problem with Vienna, since the sexual scenes, language and problems disappeared, and even Angelo was purged of his sexual desire. At the end both the Duke and Isabella were represented as an ideal pair of governors, he for his grave authority, she for her domestic and angelic virtues.

Kemble's attempt to clean up this play coincided with the efforts of Thomas Bowdler to retain and use Shakespeare as a great national treasure but to remove anything offensive (i.e. sexual). His *Family Shakespeare in Ten Volumes* was published in 1818 with a further explanation on the title page:

> … in which nothing is added to the original text; but those words and expressions are omitted which cannot with propriety be read aloud in a family.

Bowdler managed to '**bowdlerise**' the other plays, but *Measure for Measure* defeated him and he simply reprinted Kemble's acting version. The play fell out of fashion in the 19th century and was rarely performed.

From 1814 Edmund Kean (1787–1833) galvanised the London stage. He was the next great interpreter of Shakespeare and utterly different from Kemble. It was violence after dignity, a plebeian after an aristocrat and revolution after decorum. Kean embodied the Romantic age. 'To see him act', wrote the critic Hazlitt, 'is like reading Shakespeare by flashes of lightening.' Audiences flocked to see his passionate energy, but he offered far more than consummate theatricality: his innate sense of rebellion illuminated many great roles. At a performance of *The Merchant of Venice* Hazlitt expected to see Shylock 'bent with age and ugly with mental deformity'; Kean made him a poignant victim of oppression. Audiences were led to question Venice and its so-called Christian values and to make radical judgements about outsiders and the political effects of psychological bullying.

Richard III declares himself to be a villain, but Kean brought a new wild grandeur to Richard's immorality. The role derives from the medieval Vice (see above, page 32) and so there has always been tension between Richard's wickedness and his humour which engages the audience. Kean took this ambivalence to a new level. Audiences felt excited at being in a new moral world where restraint and conscience seemed not to exist. Hazlitt records that at the Battle of Bosworth, Kean's Richard fought 'like one drunk with wounds'.

Kean's early training had been in melodrama, which had none of the decorum and dignity expected of high tragedy. Melodrama used colloquial language, wild cries, extreme physicality, sudden changes of attitude and intense energy. Kean applied all these to Shakespearean tragedy, particularly to Othello's psychological pain. The poet John Keats wrote of his 'O blood, blood, Iago, blood!' that 'the very words appeared stained and gory … His voice is loosed on them like the wild dog on the savage relics of an eastern conflict.'

Kean's illumination of Shakespeare depended on brilliant moments set against the dark background of the play. In this he followed Garrick, on whose 'points', or moments of theatrical insight, rested each play's meaning. The Swiss artist Henry Fuseli (1741–1825) became fascinated by Shakespeare after seeing Garrick perform *Macbeth*. Spontaneous passion in playwright and actor led to a focus on scenes like Macbeth's meeting with the Witches, the murder of Duncan and Lady Macbeth's sleepwalking. In his illustrations, Fuseli 'staged' these moments against a dark and mysterious background, in keeping with the Gothic revival which became part of the Romantic vision in both novels and poems. He aimed to capture great moments in the performances of Garrick and Kean, but his works go beyond the theatre and into his own imaginative experience of 'the sublime', an idealised form of terror which *Macbeth*, of all Shakespeare's plays, most vividly explores.

By now Shakespeare was communicated through the proscenium picture frame of the theatre, and more sophisticated lighting was being introduced. These changes allowed for stage illusion that had been impossible on the open stage of Shakespeare's time. Then the audiences had seen each other as well as the performance in afternoon daylight. Then the theatre experience had been communal; but now, with Kean and Fuseli, it was moving towards private intensity and our world of the cinema. It is not surprising that Fuseli was particularly fascinated by *Macbeth* and *A Midsummer Night's Dream*, both of which are set mostly at night-time. Moments of light against the darkness, as well as being visually powerful in the theatre, are metaphorically part of the Romantic actor's method.

The 19th century: Victorian grandeur

Queen Victoria reigned from 1837 to 1901. As queen she chose to embody family and domestic virtues, but her statesmen and industrialists built up the wealthiest empire the world had ever known. To continue as national icon Shakespeare now had to represent both unblemished morality and ambitious national confidence. Edmund Kean's unstable passions were too disturbing to exemplify these qualities. The great actors who followed Kean – William Macready at the start of Victoria's reign and Henry Irving at the end – were more dignified and restrained.

Staging Shakespeare

Victorian productions of Shakespeare were carefully researched for period accuracy. Charles Kean (son of Edmund) devoted himself and his theatre to this task. In 1857 he was elected as a Fellow of the Royal Society of Antiquaries. He researched not the Elizabethan period of Shakespeare, but the period in which the stories are notionally set: ancient Britain for *King Lear*, 11th-century Scotland for *Macbeth*, the late Middle Ages for *Richard III*. Sets and costumes dominated so strongly that, in a sense, all Shakespeare's plays became history plays. There was more rehearsal, more drilling of the crowd scenes, more attention given to sound and lighting effects.

The first half of the century continued the traditional arrangements of wings and flats cut into grooves in the stage floor with an upstage variety of backdrops. Actors still performed downstage of this two-dimensional scenery, but after 1870 Henry Irving introduced more solid three-dimensional pieces through which actors could move. He also employed some of the country's major artists to design and paint them. Another popular piece of scenery was the diorama, a cloth with different scenes painted on it; lighting the diorama either changed the atmosphere of the scenes or moved from one to another to give an illusion of travel. Victorian lighting methods were limited but effective – certainly less spectacular than the scenery. Gas replaced oil lamps in 1815; limelight was first used at Covent Garden in 1837, and electric lighting, with its vast potential, was first attempted in 1881.

Above all, the productions were pictorial, and often long and cumbersome because of the time taken to move heavy scenery. Charles Kean's *The Tempest* required 140 stage hands. *Julius Caesar*, a short play as we know it, was divided into three acts with major intervals between. There was also the fashion for 'tableaux vivants', the action frozen for a time, while the actors created a still picture of a telling moment. In addition, each act would end with a stage picture that embodied a strand of the play's meaning, even if this meant rearranging the lines; the picture was intended to linger in the audience's memory as darkness fell. For a moment the theatre had become an art gallery. In reverse, there are also many Victorian paintings that imitate the stage, capturing a climax: Hamlet with Yorick's skull, Malvolio posturing before Olivia in *Twelfth Night*. Victorian culture, whether exclusive or popular, was highly visual, and also aware of the messages of history. So Shakespeare became a playwright-historian whose works, when turned into elaborate pictures, would educate morality and support national self-esteem.

Victorian audiences enjoyed the opulent effects. But it would be wrong to dismiss Victorian trends simply because we have come to value nimble staging and sparse décor. Audiences today also enjoy cinema and lavish musicals with their huge casts and terrifying costs; these art forms have inherited the priorities of large-scale 19th-century entertainment. The Victorians believed in spending time, money and heroic efforts to build a great empire. They made a similar commitment to preserve and express the works of 'the world's greatest playwright' – especially as good fortune had made him English!

Shakespeare began to reach a wider audience. London companies visited other areas of the country. Improved transport made touring profitable and a few celebrated productions could be played more often. There was also trans-Atlantic touring: Irving went to America eight times and Macready twice. American actors came to London, notably Edwin Booth with *Hamlet* and Ada Rehan as Rosalind. In London the then unfashionable Sadlers Wells under Samuel Phelps's management staged most of Shakespeare's plays between 1844 and 1862. This was a remarkable undertaking: his audiences were chiefly tradespeople and clerks, and even in the main theatre areas of London barely one-third of Shakespeare's 37 plays were regularly shown.

The relative popularity of some plays may surprise us. *King John, Henry VIII* and *The Merry Wives of Windsor* are rarely performed today. For the Victorians, they conveyed a stronger sense of Shakespeare, the English playwright, than our favourite sequence, the tetralogy (four plays) of *Richard II, Henry IV Parts 1 and 2* and *Henry V. King Lear* was too intimidating to be often performed, though Macready's landmark production in 1838 returned to Shakespeare's version after 150 years of Nahum Tate's (see page 46 above). Audiences were at last able to appreciate the importance of the Fool, not included since Shakespeare's time. As had become common with androgynous or strange male roles, it was played by a young actress.

Interpretations of Shakespeare: Irving and Ellen Terry

Great actors were aware of carrying the Shakespearean torch: from Burbage to Betterton, Garrick, Kean, Macready and Irving. The famous Victorian actors were also managers, with often dictatorial control over every aspect of their theatres. They took the financial risks, controlled the programming of a season, the casting, staging and design of the productions. Above all, they ensured that the core of the play was their own star performance.

As women in a patriarchal age, actresses rarely had any influence in management. But, since Sarah Siddons at the turn of the century, actresses could also draw the audiences. Helen Faucit (with Macready) and Ellen Terry (with Irving) were the most celebrated.

Particular roles became a sort of trademark. Ellen Terry gave what seemed to be definitive performances as Imogen in *Cymbeline* and as Lady Macbeth. She enjoyed a creative partnership with Irving, which could also become competitive. The great art critic, John Ruskin, wrote to Irving after seeing his Shylock and her Portia in 1879:

> I felt … that you were a most true and noble and tender actor – but you had not yet as much love for Shakespeare as for your art, and were therefore not careful enough to be wholly in harmony with his design … and though Miss Terry's Portia has obtained so much applause, it greatly surprises me that you have not taught her a grander reading of the part. Portia is chiefly great in her majestic humility (the main sign of her splendid intellect) and – to take only one instance of what I do not doubt to be misinterpretation – the speech, 'You see me, Lord Bassanio …' she would, I am certain, produce its true effect on the audience only if spoken with at least half a dozen yards between her and Bassanio – and with her eyes on the ground through most of the lines.

In general, Victorian theatre criticism was an undeveloped skill: most reviews were highly personal, either fawning on a great actor or savagely cutting down an opponent. Ruskin's views here are written in a private letter and suggest some interesting attitudes:

- a gentle rebuke to Irving for using Shakespeare to boost his own star status

- a concern for the meaning of the play as a whole, for the 'harmony' of Shakespeare's design

- the expectation that the actor-manager will teach his company, perhaps combining the duties of today's director and drama school (as well as playing the lead role himself)

- a rather dogmatic insistence on the externals of stage 'business' (a 20th-century method actor would object to 'half a dozen yards' and 'eyes on the ground' as ways to convey artistic truth)

- a concern for 'intellect' in the actress and the character she plays.

It was probably shrewd of Ruskin to mention 'intellect', because Irving wanted to raise the status of acting to that of other intellectual activities. Irving was invited to see an undergraduate production at Balliol College in Oxford and afterwards spoke to one of the young actors, F.R. Benson (who later became famous with his own company):

> You young men did splendidly. If only I had had the opportunity in my young days that you have in yours! … We have the technical skill on the stage, we have the traditions; the difficulty nowadays is to get a company that has the literary mind and the trained intellectuality that is associated with university students.

In the second half of the 20th century, Irving belatedly had his wish, when most of the new young directors and many of the actors came from the leading universities, with the 'Cambridge mafia' most prominent. If their approach to Shakespeare was criticised, it was often for wilful gimmickry, for gratuitous innovation. But in the 1870s Irving was expected to maintain traditions. His *Hamlet*, which ran for an extraordinary 200 performances, was the more remarkable for Irving's seeing the role in a fresh light. Clement Scott, a serious critic at the *Daily Telegraph*, reviewing the first performance in 1874, wrote that Irving cast 'an indescribable spell' over an audience predisposed to criticise, that 'here was the Hamlet who thinks aloud; here was the scholar and so little of the actor'.

▶ Which of the plays that you know do most (and least) to support a Victorian ideal of Shakespeare providing good moral instruction to readers and audiences?

▶ The 1890s director Beerbohm Tree defended himself against the criticism that his popular productions of Shakespeare cheapened great plays: 'Thousands witness him instead of hundreds. His works are not only, or primarily, for the literary student, they are for the world at large. Indeed there should be more joy over ninety-nine Philistines that are gained than over one elect that is preserved.' What is your view of his defence?

Towards the 20th century: back to the source

Four events at the end of the 19th century helped to shape radical thinking about how to stage Shakespeare:

- 1881 – William Poel's amateur production of the first Quarto version of *Hamlet* in an 'Elizabethan' style

- 1888 – the discovery in Germany of de Witt's 1596 drawing of the Swan Theatre, the only eyewitness picture of an Elizabethan theatre interior

- 1894 – the foundation of the Elizabethan Stage Society: to revive 'the masterpieces of the Elizabethan drama upon the stage for which they were written'

- 1904 – the publication by W.W. Greg of Philip Henslowe's diaries and papers (see Part 1, page 11)

Re-creating Shakespeare: William Poel

Poel (1852–1934) was a scholar, with limited talent as a director, who rejected the lavish pictorial effects of Victorian Shakespeare. In particular, he objected to the picture-frame proscenium which separated actors from the audience. Sir Henry Irving at The Lyceum Theatre was the eminent Victorian actor-manager whose productions embodied these values. Poel wrote: 'I wouldn't give him five pounds a week. He is wonderful in his way, but it is not my way.'

Poel couldn't build new theatres, but he tried to create Elizabethan conditions within existing ones. These were based on a permanent uncluttered stage with no extra scenery, using Elizabethan period costume, rapid playing without intervals and a rhythmic continuity of action. He restored those brief scenes (like the Porter in *Macbeth*) which seemed to the Victorians to contradict the play's overall mood. Poel's *Hamlet* was an unlocalised and timeless action. He restored Fortinbras and removed much of Irving's sentimental interpretation of 1874. Hamlet was now volatile and difficult, not the romantic, noble prince.

Poel attended more to the play's structure and the music of the language than to finding deep or rounded character. The actor and director Sir Lewis Casson (1875–1969) wrote that Poel's 'first step was to cast the play orchestrally. He decided which character represented the double bass, the cello, the woodwind … and chose actors by the timbre, pitch and flexibility of their voices.'

There were some limitations. Poel's stages could not achieve the full Elizabethan platform design: he could manage only an apron stage that pushed through the proscenium across the orchestra pit, and so an actor could not make the powerful downstage movement to command the centre of the building. His stages were generally surrounded with curtains, which gave an austere impression, unlike the theatre of 1600; but they certainly made their protest against Victorian picture sets.

There was a more philosophical limitation. Poel was substituting one type of 'archaeology' for another: the Victorians had researched the period settings for each play, whereas his scholarly 'digging' was into the theatre of 1600. But, however accurate his researches, he could not re-create the audiences of 1600, their lives, habits and beliefs, as they responded to Shakespeare for the first time. Details of costume in 1600, for example, could hold messages that in 1900 only programme notes could reveal. If theatre is an act of live communication (performers to audience), the success of Poel and his followers must be limited if they can research and change only the performers' half of the communication. In a sense, therefore, this type of reconstruction of Shakespeare must run the danger of putting him in a museum.

There was one way, however, in which Poel helped to fulfil Irving's wishes. Irving hoped that raising the status of actors would bring in the universities (see page 56, above). Poel's researches led to partnerships in the 20th century between scholars and actors, which helped towards establishing the new prominent role of director. Scholars became less inclined to dismiss the theatre for its crude popular appeal. There was less emphasis on Shakespeare as a sublime poet and more on his practical **stagecraft**, more awareness that he must be read with performance in mind. In a broadcast in 1937, the scholar John Dover Wilson said: 'Never believe what the scholars and professors tell you about a Shakespeare play until you have seen it on stage for yourself.'

The 20th century: the director appears

Three major influences emerged at the start of the 20th century:

- Poel's principles of a return to Elizabethan practice (see page 57, above), leading to the emergence of directors such as Barker and Guthrie.

- Edward Gordon Craig's pioneering design principles (see page 60, below). His mystical, abstract creations were a world away from the Victorian historical picture frame.

- The scholar A.C. Bradley's publication of *Shakespearean Tragedy* in 1904, treating characters in tragedy as if they were real human beings who live in worlds familiar to us.

Early modern directors: Barker and Guthrie

In the early years of the 20th century, the greatest theatre director was Harley Granville Barker. Barker's Shakespeare productions at the Savoy Theatre broke new ground. Starting with *The Winter's Tale* in 1912, Barker merged the views of Poel and Bradley. When speaking of Poel's 'fine fanaticism', Barker was praising his principles but trying to avoid an overdogmatic use of them in the theatre.

Like Poel, Barker abandoned footlights, painted canvases and the Victorians' belief in faithful historical representation. As far as possible, he brought the play's action onto an apron stage in front of the proscenium arch. He tried to achieve intimacy with the audience, continuity from scene to scene, pace, and musical variety in the verse-speaking. In a letter to the *Daily Mail* he wrote: 'I abide by the text and the demands of the text, and beyond that I claim freedom.'

Unlike Poel, Barker believed in flexible invention of design; he chose simple abstract settings that could reflect light and suggest space. His production of *A Midsummer Night's Dream* in 1914 shocked traditionalist critics because of his new thinking about the fairy world. The fairies were not charming balletic children, but adults with individual characteristics that suggested a complete fairy community. Barker's notes in his script refer to a 'doctor', 'professor', 'ecclesiastic', an 'old man fairy'. They were all dressed in gold; there were masks and Indian headdresses. The fairies communicated in strange mechanical gestures. Bottom, Quince and the other 'mechanicals' were not slapstick clowns, but believable countrymen from Warwickshire.

Barker was the first of the modern directors, a role that had never existed in or since Shakespeare's day. There had been managers and leading actors, and in the 19th century a succession of autocratic actor-managers who controlled the rudimentary artistic policy. But Barker led the way towards what we have come to know as 'director's theatre', where one man (until recent years it was very rarely a woman) casts the play, studies and interprets it and controls all decisions about design, props, lighting and all stage effects.

Later in the century, the director Tyrone Guthrie brought a new influence to productions of Shakespeare. In some ways he followed Poel in presenting Shakespeare on an uncluttered open stage, but used the space with more beautifully choreographed freedom. Unlike Poel, he believed that 'all performance is equally a comment upon, as well as a recreation of, the work performed'. His Festival Theatre in Ontario, Canada, became a workshop for his theories on performing Shakespeare and influenced the design of new theatres in England, notably the Chichester Festival Theatre in 1962 and The Crucible Theatre in Sheffield in 1971. Guthrie rejected artificial divisions of the plays into acts and scenes, seeing Shakespeare as an organic whole with great rhythmic variety; for him the differences of prose/verse, private/public, intimate/ceremonial allowed for constantly changing focus. Although his productions included depth of character, he was praised for their heightened, non-illusory qualities. The word 'ritual' was often applied to his work. In this he anticipated the even bolder work of Peter Brook (see page 68, below).

Space and design: Edward Gordon Craig and his influence

Edward Gordon Craig was the first great stage designer of the 20th century. He was the son of the actress Ellen Terry and after a short period as an actor he specialised in stage design, especially for dance. He believed that space, light and movement were at the heart of interpreting a play. He was less interested in language – and was at times accused of turning actors into puppets who would merely contribute to a visual experience. He had a mystical, almost religious concept of theatre that sometimes by-passed practical concerns. But he influenced future production design by his view that the designer should pick one or two dominant images from the play and let these images symbolise the whole. This could convey the unity of a Shakespeare play:

> Come now, we take *Macbeth* … In what kind of place is that play laid? I see two things. I see a lofty and steep rock, and I see the moist cloud which envelops the head of this rock. That is to say, a place for fierce and warlike men to inhabit, a place for phantoms to nest in. Ultimately this moisture will destroy the rock; ultimately those spirits will destroy the men.

After poor reviews in England, Craig spent most of his creative life in Germany, but was invited to The Moscow Arts Theatre by the great director Stanislavski to both direct and design a production of *Hamlet* in 1912. It was an odd invitation because Stanislavski was a pioneer in working closely with his company to explore motivation and psychology, an approach which led to the American school of method acting. Not surprisingly the actors resented Craig and eventually Stanislavski had to take over as director.

Craig's stylised approach can be inferred from his notes for the design of the first scene:

> The problem is to show the throne, the three characters *(the King, Queen and Hamlet)* and the retinue, the courtiers, merge into one generalised background of gold. Their mantles flow together, and they cannot be perceived to have individual faces. They are rough brush-strokes, saturated with majesty, a background.

The eventual design impressed audiences but fell short of Craig's intentions and (for a different reason) Stanislavski's. Stanislavski remembered it some years later:

> … its beauty attacked the eye and hid the actors in its pomp. This new quality of the stage was a surprise to me. The more we tried to make the production simple, the stronger it reminded us of itself, the more it seemed pretentious and displayed its showy naïvete.

Craig was highly imaginative, with a refreshing disregard for convention, but he had mixed fortunes as a practising designer. Like Poel as a director (see page 57, above), he was too inflexible in his working methods, but both were pioneers who are best remembered as influential theorists.

Later 20th-century designers owed much to Craig, even when they didn't imitate his individual style. He swept away the need for illusion, naturalism and historical research. Design could now suggest an abstract mood rather than imitate surfaces. Light, space and texture could be more valuable than intricate detail. Design must also respond to the theatre, the playing space and its relationship to the audience. Some directors have disliked theatres, with their rigid internal design, and have preferred spaces that are 'almost theatres', like tents, cellars, pubs and warehouses. These can seem to offer more scope for improvisation, for a return to simple storytelling, for what Peter Brook calls 'rough theatre'.

The director Charles Marowitz, then assistant to Brook, created a 'Lear log' for their 1962 production (see page 68, below). He describes the elemental look of the stage:

> The set consists of geometrical sheets which are ginger with rust and corrosion. The costumes, dominantly leather, have been textured to suggest long and hard wear. The knights' tabards are peeling with long use; Lear's cape and coat are creased and blackened with time and weather. The furniture is hard wood, once sturdy, but now decaying back into hard, brown grain. Apart from the rust, the leather and the old wood, there is nothing but space – giant white flats opening on to a blank cyclorama [a white, curved backcloth at the rear of the stage].

It was once assumed that Shakespeare's massive histories and tragedies needed the dignity of large theatres and expensive design. Now directors and designers think more flexibly. Smaller spaces and smaller financial budgets have shown that plays like *King Lear* and *Antony and Cleopatra* can reveal new aspects of their meaning when their staging and design are pared down. Powerful visual design can be achieved simply in seeing actors on stage in their changing patterns of movement and grouping. They can be supported by further design in lighting and sound effects, either live or recorded, and by simple objects, props and fabrics.

► Consider Craig's view that a designer should focus on one or two strong images. Choose any Shakespeare plays you know well and list a maximum of three images which might lead to one of Craig's designs.

Later 20th century: director's theatre

20th- and 21st-century directors have taken increasingly more freedom to interpret the plays afresh. Some critics have argued that they do this not to serve the play but to introduce gimmickry that will bring publicity for them and their careers. From the 1960s onwards, the theatre and opera director Jonathan Miller has had to face some of this criticism, and in his book *Subsequent Performances* he acknowledges that there must be limits to a director's possible interpretations. When does fresh interpretation become a self-indulgent wrenching of the play? He cites a line from *Hamlet*: when the king is praying he begins with, 'O my offence is rank'. It would be perverse, Miller argues, not to see this as a murderer's guilt for his crime. However, the actor can still play the guilt in different ways. These depend on attitudes to the king and Hamlet that have built up in the first three acts of the play: is the king trying hard to be responsible in guiding the state of Denmark or has he been merely self-indulgent in enjoying his throne and queen? Is Hamlet more cruel than kind, or the opposite? And the king's line itself can be spoken in different ways: with a sigh, with angry self-disgust, with clinical self-analysis.

▶ Take any short passage (e.g. two or more lines) from a Shakespeare play you know well and prepare to speak as many legitimate interpretations as possible. Try to find a dividing line that separates what is unusual and justifiable from what is unusual and perverse.

Miller believes that 'there is a sense in which a play can be said to have been completed only when work has been supplied by someone other than the playwright'. If the play is constantly performed over 400 years, as many of Shakespeare's have been, then it must be assumed that he would be happy for control to have slipped away from him and into the hands of the director and company who are performing it. This process may sound like a loss, but Miller believes it to be a gain:

> By submitting to the possibility of successive re-creation, the play passes through the development that is its birthright, and its meaning begins to be fully appreciated only when it enters a period that I shall call its afterlife.

After 1960 Shakespeare's 'afterlife' saw a vigorous and rapid growth in some startling directions. It is hard to give exact reasons for this, but some social influences contributed, for example:

- A sense of needing a new start in post-war Britain brought an impatience with genteel middle-class 'drawing-room' theatre.

- Drab times of hardship and rationing in the late 1940s were followed by drama schools producing rough, gutsy actors and by playwrights offering them 'kitchen sink' plays and films.

- Psychoanalysis (especially the theories of Freud) encouraged theatre's investigation of the troubled subconscious (see Part 3, page 75).

- Close textual scrutiny in the universities (F.R. Leavis, for example, at Cambridge) encouraged a number of bright, articulate young directors, many of whom had studied English Literature, not Drama.

Many directors specialised in being sceptical and uncomfortable. It seemed to some critics, unhappy with these new trends, that directors had become brutally perverse, believing (so it seemed) that offering reassurance to an audience must be shallow sentimentality, whereas to disturb them must be an obvious sign of intelligence. Sometimes this edgy scepticism was a conscious comment on the political and social conditions around them. As Britain lost its empire, it seemed to become a diminished force. People questioned what being British meant, and Shakespeare could no longer represent nobility, Englishness and patriotism.

Audiences used to more predictable productions of Shakespeare in the 1930s and 1940s found their expectations challenged by the new directors of the 1960s and later. Here are some typical examples:

- In *Hamlet* Ophelia, once sweet, docile and beautiful, might now be neurotic and unpredictable with a relish for being sexually explicit.

- In Jonathan Miller's *The Merchant of Venice* the trial was held in drab legal chambers instead of grand public opulence. He wrote: 'I recoiled from the sentimental radiance that actresses bring to Portia's mercy speech'.

- Ariel in *The Tempest* is no longer a balletic sprite, but may be ugly, immobile and resentful.

- *Much Ado About Nothing* can end not with a joyful dance but with the captured Don John dragged onto the stage and shot.

- In *King Lear* the Fool might be any sort of alien outsider instead of a pert young boy; sometimes (as in Jonathan Miller's 1982 BBC production) he is an old man of Lear's age.

- In Peter Hall's production of *Henry V* (with Ian Holm) 'the noble patriot had been successfully usurped by an energetic runt'.

The history of Shakespeare in 20th-century theatre has celebrated great actors, as it always has – names like Gielgud, Olivier, Redgrave, Ashcroft, Dench, McKellen,

Jacobi. But unlike the first 300 years of Shakespeare's 'afterlife', directors have become just as important, even though they are not seen on stage to be applauded. Barker, Barry Jackson of the Birmingham Rep, and Guthrie dominated the first 50 years of the 20th century. Since then Peter Hall, Peter Brook and Trevor Nunn have been innovators and leaders for 50 years of astonishing creative stamina. Nicholas Hytner, Gregory Doran, Sam Mendes, Michael Boyd are younger directors, all with impressive track records, all doing much of their greatest work for The Royal Shakespeare Company or the National Theatre.

Some directors have become well-known for seeming to do very little. Declan Donnellan with his designer Nick Ormrod founded the Cheek by Jowl theatre company in 1981. It has become one of the most thoughtfully inventive companies in recent years. Their manifesto was to re-examine classical texts (with Shakespeare at the core), to focus on the actor's art and to avoid concepts imposed by the director. Their work is always vivid, clear, physical and searching for the inner truth of a play without aiming for traditional coherence of set, costume, time or place. In 1991 they celebrated their tenth year with a remarkable production of *As You Like It*, which was both playful and profound. On the surface it was 'authentic' Shakespeare in that all the roles were played by men, but it treated gender in a way that was radical for its time in that it avoided the danger of camp posturing. It convinced audiences that male and female were gender roles that could be adopted and discarded at will. The production impressed the critic John Peter, who wrote that the play 'is not about sexuality – hetero-, homo-, bi- or trans – but about love, which both transcends sexuality and includes it'. (See extract in Part 4, page 95.)

The Royal Shakespeare Company

In 1960 when Peter Hall arrived in Stratford to manage the Shakespeare Memorial Theatre Company one of his first decisions was to change its name to The Royal Shakespeare Company. 'Memorial' suggested reverence, as though seeing Shakespeare on stage was like visiting a heritage museum. His successor, Trevor Nunn, remembers that 'audiences arrived in Stratford very much as if they were on a pilgrimage'.

A permanent theatre to honour Shakespeare was first built in Stratford in 1879. It was a Victorian Gothic building which burnt down after 50 years and was replaced in 1932. Two more theatres were later added: a studio theatre-in-the-round, The Other Place, in 1974 and The Swan Theatre, with an Elizabethan-style thrust stage, in 1986. These three very different theatre spaces not only enabled different styles of Shakespeare production but also extended Hall's policy of a permanent ensemble company that would stage new writing and other classics as well as Shakespeare. Today the 1932 theatre has been found inadequate: it is inflexible, too like cinema architecture, imposing a barrier of distance between stage and audience. By 2010 it will have been radically altered.

There has been much change since 1960. Hall insisted that the plays must be 'relevant' to each year's audiences, but that this aim did not mean that they had to be 'topical' in the sense of being closely linked to whatever events and issues dominate the current news. Hall also disliked imposing a single dominating idea or a historical period on a play:

> I cannot bear people who do Shakespeare with 'concepts'. A concept is usually like an extreme article in some learned publication about one tiny aspect of the play. It puts blinkers on the play.

Hall was aware of each play's historical and cultural origins. While still wanting creative freedom for the actors and designers, he also wanted a **Renaissance** reference in the costume to anchor the plays to the world they were created in.

Now, nearly 50 years after Hall began managing the RSC, the wilder creativity of some younger directors who have followed him to Stratford has sometimes made him seem old-fashioned. Such criticism is perhaps unfair, but it shows that theatre is subject to fashion as young artists arrive eager to prove their individuality. Hall has been targeted chiefly for his highly disciplined attitude to Shakespeare's verse; one critic called him an 'iambic fundamentalist'. But Hall believes that discipline and freedom are not polar opposites: they must coexist and reinforce each other. He is also a highly successful director of opera, and often refers to Shakespeare's heightened language as though it is music:

> There is a great deal to be learned from the text in notation, almost as much as in a musical score … Blank verse is a form, just as singing is a form. These are … artificial means of shaping naturalistic behaviour and speech, giving them a form which enables us to deal with emotions and attitudes and responses which might be too painful or even ridiculous for us if they were done naturalistically.

Landmark productions of the 1960s

Hall's creative mixture of freedom and discipline were evident in two landmark productions in the 1960s. *The Wars of the Roses* was a partnership with the scholar and director John Barton, who created a trilogy of plays from Shakespeare's four early histories, *Henry VI Parts 1, 2, 3* and *Richard III*. Some purists felt that huge liberties were taken, akin to 17th-century adaptations (see pages 45–46, above), in that Barton cut huge stretches of the plays and wrote his own 'Shakespearean' linking verse. But there was great critical acclaim at the same time, and since then there have been several historical groupings, performed by a single company (often with very creative doubling) including the Roman plays in 1973, at Stratford, directed by Hall's successor, Trevor Nunn. Hall himself had directed *Hamlet* in 1965 with David Warner as the prince. Audiences remembered this production long afterwards as a modern production in line with protest movements of the 1960s. Warner's Hamlet was callow, and juvenile: he wore a long scarf making him look like students of that period, and, like some students, he switched between being a drop-out and a political activist. But those same audiences were often surprised to be reminded that it was costumed as a Renaissance play. The critic Ronald Bryden saw it not as an imperfect play but as 'the perfected tragedy of an unfinished hero':

> For the revenge he really wishes, and achieves, is on himself for not being the great Hamlet his father was. The key to every *Hamlet* is its ghost. A solid ghost demands an active, believing hero, thwarted by events; an insubstantial one, all light-effects and echoes, a brainsick prince, nerveless and Oedipal. The apparition which swims above the walls of John Bury's Elsinore (a superb inferno of bitumen ramparts and lakes of black marble...) is something new: a giant, helmeted shadow ten feet tall which dwarfs his shuddering child in a dark, commanding embrace. 'This was a man,' Hamlet tells Horatio enviously: for once we are shown the other side of the Oedipus complex. This Hamlet is less jealous of his mother's bedfellow than of his father's stature.
>
> (Ronald Bryden in the *New Statesman*, 27 August 1965)

▶ Does this review put greater emphasis on the acting or the staging of Peter Hall's production?

Later landmark productions

In the 19th century, *The Tempest* held little appeal for the Victorian actor-managers because Prospero seemed to be a passionless sage representing the controlling authority of Shakespeare. After Darwin's theories of evolution, Caliban was interpreted as a sort of missing link between ape and man and, in some productions, he provided the main dramatic interest. In the 20th century, *The Tempest* has become more popular. Since the 1960s, the RSC has led the way to more complex reassessments that have explored the possibilities of a mutinous Ariel and a sympathetic Caliban, both subject to a Prospero who imposes authority without mastering his own inner turbulence. There can be many different approaches to playing Prospero. Directors and actors generally feel they have to make choices. But Nick Hytner's direction of John Wood as Prospero at the RSC in 1988 didn't simply decide between serene philosopher and volatile, angry duke: together director and actor aimed to incorporate almost everything that the writing can suggest. Christine Dymkowski in her book on the stage history of *The Tempest* (see Part 6, page 120,) described the performance:

> … moving easily between Prospero the thoughtless task-master, the gentle guardian, the outraged aristocrat, the socially inept man, the loving father, the blinkered judge of past actions, the lonely child still carried within the adult being, Wood gave a performance that can serve as a summary of the role's possibilities in the late 20th century.

Other critics felt the mixture too confusing, some claiming that Wood's rapid switches led to inaudible delivery which damaged the poetry. However, the intention indicated an RSC determination to explore the text carefully. It also highlights the danger that modern approaches can risk incoherence when they abandon a single overall reading in favour of one which welcomes variety, even clashes. Some directors instruct the actors to play each scene as it comes. If one contradicts the next, so be it: life itself is muddled, plays may imitate this aspect of life, and it is not the job of actors to tidy up either life or art.

Macbeth also deals with the supernatural and, like *The Tempest*, can break with tradition and work powerfully on a bare stage. The RSC has become a versatile institution and has welcomed different playing spaces. The Swan comes closest to Shakespeare's Globe, but the smaller theatres, The Other Place and (for a time) the Donmar Warehouse in London, have been used for the 'great' plays. The Victorians, eager for decorum, wanted large theatres and spectacular effects for *Macbeth*, which is Shakespeare's most complete and searching treatment of evil. But Trevor Nunn's RSC production in 1976 drove the play not outward into the military culture of ancient Scotland, but deep into the minds of Macbeth and his wife (played by Ian McKellen and Judi Dench). A small audience of about 200 sat three-quarters round an inner circle of 14 actors sitting on beer crates. Within this empty circle was the intense action of the play. There was no set, few props, simple, dark costumes of no special period and a sense of oppressive and unrelieved darkness. There was no interval and the entire playing time lasted barely above two hours. The whole focus was given to the actors so that the effect was like being in a laboratory probing the nature of evil, and what it felt like for husband and wife to experience a state of living damnation. Some critics regretted the loss of armies and the battle which delivers Scotland from its nightmare; instead voices and sound effects surrounded Macbeth. The ending gave no sense of triumph or restored order. The successful army slumped like exhausted survivors while Malcolm, more shaken than victorious, gave orders for his coronation.

Peter Brook and 'The Empty Space'

Two of the greatest challenges to audience preconceptions were productions by Peter Brook, who arrived at Stratford in 1946 at the age of 21. His greatest innovations with Shakespeare were *King Lear* (1962) and *A Midsummer Night's Dream* (1970). He was influenced by the Polish critic, Jan Kott, whose book *Shakespeare Our Contemporary* saw the plays in terms of bleak mid-century European politics and the equally bleak plays of Samuel Beckett.

Brook's *King Lear* was a powerful metaphysical experience, often including nihilist farce. The king, played by Paul Scofield, was a blunt, grizzled warrior; Kent was a bully and the knights were destructive hooligans. Goneril and Regan seemed at first to represent civilised values as they tried to impose some order and graciousness to a grim competitive world. Only later did their cruelty appear. Brook offended some critics by omitting the hushed event that follows Gloucester's blinding at the end of Act 3: no servants came forward to show tenderness after the horrible torture. Instead the white house lights suddenly blazed out; members of the audience saw each other and the stagehands clearing the debris – and amongst these mundane details, the blinded old man crawled towards the wings.

By contrast, Brook's *A Midsummer Night's Dream* was an exuberant celebration, but not within a historical period or in ways that an audience could easily recognise. The company had searched for a more individual way of staging magic that could allow the imagination to range rapidly through joy, alarm, mystery and even surreal farce. Everything was played within a white box, the actors were physically adept, as much performers as characters. Oberon and Puck played some of their scenes on trapezes, their purple flower containing the love juice was expressed as a spinning plate poised delicately on a juggler's wand and was then flipped from one to the other high above the stage level. Actors not part of a particular scene watched from above and contributed atmospheric sounds. The play's magic worked on the imagination but concealed nothing of how it was created. This was a joyful performer's theatre requiring extreme contribution from the audience. At the end Puck raced through the theatre shaking hands: 'Give me your hands if we be friends.' Shakespeare's company would not have presented the play like this in the 1590s, yet most critics agreed that the production had found the celebratory spirit of the writing and should not be categorised merely as a display of director's ingenuity.

In 1968 Brook wrote his influential book, *The Empty Space*, in which he explains with great simplicity some of his profound thoughts about theatre. Like Poel and his successors, Brook valued the 'empty space' of Shakespeare's stage:

> What has not been appreciated sufficiently is that the freedom
> of movement of the Elizabethan theatre was not only a matter of

scenery. It is too easy to think that so long as a modern production moves fast from scene to scene, it has learned the essential lesson from the old playhouse. The primary fact is that this theatre not only allowed the playwright to roam the world, it also allowed him free passage from the world of action to the world of inner impressions. I think it is here that we find what is most important to us today. In Shakespeare's time, the voyage of discovery in the real world, the adventure of the traveller setting out into the unknown, had an excitement that we cannot hope to capture in an age when our planet has no secrets and when the prospect of interplanetary travel seems a pretty considerable bore. However, Shakespeare was not satisfied with the mysteries of the unknown continents: through his imagery – pictures drawn from the world of fabulous discoveries – he penetrates a psychic existence whose geography and movements remain just as vital for us to understand today.

▶ How well has any Shakespeare production you have seen moved from what Brook describes as 'the world of action' to 'the world of inner impressions'? Do you agree with Brook's estimate of the differences and similarities between Shakespeare's time and our own?

The Globe Theatre

Throughout the 20th century there have been attempts, especially in America, to build replica Elizabethan theatres and to reconstruct Shakespeare's methods. There has been research into Elizabethan pronunciation and even into formulaic gestures which actors may have used to signify emotions and attitudes. The most important achievement in Britain has been the construction and successful running of Shakespeare's Globe Theatre in Southwark, the district on the south bank of the Thames which in 1600 had been such a teeming area of life and entertainment. Modern development has revived this part of London: the huge Tate Modern gallery, the nearby National Theatre, the Millennium Bridge connecting with St Paul's Cathedral on the north bank, the cafés, restaurants and riverside walkways. Theatre always related to its local community and after London's great fire in 1666 fashionable life had shifted to the west, including the West End theatre area centring on Shaftesbury Avenue. Today the City, London's basis for work and wealth, and (downriver) the new Docklands development, have helped shift the focus away from the West End back to 'real' life in the south and east.

Shakespeare's Globe, since its opening in 1995, has become a fixture on the cultural tourist route and also a 'laboratory' for experiment and change. All aspects of the 1599 Globe have been researched: architecture, building materials, costume, music, styles of acting. Mark Rylance, the first director, also led the way in showing how actors could relate to audiences in such an unfamiliar space. It became clear that no play would be 'ready' for the first night in the sense of rehearsals reaching their end. In the old tradition of playing extempore, each performance is a sort of rehearsal and includes great flexibility: in delivering lines, playing to an audience, positioning and moves on stage.

The Globe's productions have received a mixed press. Some critics feel that comedy there, especially when slapstick, has flourished in a robust way, but that tragedies have been less successful. Audience participation, it seems, is more difficult to encourage and exploit in tragedy. Audiences sometimes find it hard to relax and respond to the types of stimulus that tragedy includes. Sometimes they have been overeager to act as Elizabethans; but, unlike the companies, the audiences have no opportunity to research a genuine Elizabethan ambience. If they are self-conscious in playing their role as groundlings, the actors then have to respond to the clumsy 'acting' from the auditorium.

Parts of some plays can benefit from this danger. *Henry V* (performed in The Globe's first season) dramatises a clear contrast between the war-weary English troops and the sneeringly overconfident French. It was easy for the actors playing French noblemen before Agincourt to direct their abuse to the groundlings, who then stood for Henry's army and were encouraged to boo and hiss in reply.

The ending was also powerful, but more subtle in the way it used the daylit, illusionless stage: Henry and Katherine left as king and queen under a shower of confetti, the Chorus spoke the Epilogue, then the whole company returned to perform a robust jig, accompanied by drumming with staves. Each actor was still dressed partly as their character but had shed part of the costume. Like Prospero at the end of *The Tempest*, they were partly players and partly the role they had played. The joyful lift at the end of the story provided the context for this half-teasing, half-mysterious playing with illusion.

Actors have found the experience of acting at Shakespeare's Globe illuminating and very different from traditional indoor proscenium theatres:

- 'It's a wonderful story-telling space. It's very easy to listen here.'

- 'You need a lot of energy … it's a sort of joyful energy.'

- 'Sound is a more powerful tool in staging at The Globe than sight.'

- 'When actors come to the front of the stage they look like giants.'

- 'The key is to keep the language alive without allowing it to be declamatory.'

- 'This is obviously a story – I'm not allowed to pretend it isn't.'

3 | Critical approaches

- What factors influence the choice of period in which to set a play?

- How far can tampering with the texts of the plays be justified?

- In what ways have critical and theoretical trends influenced productions?

- Should productions seek to present a single, unified view of a play?

The play's setting: period or modern?

A breakthrough in staging occurred in 1925, when the director Barry Jackson saw Birmingham schoolchildren perform the mechanicals' scenes from *A Midsummer Night's Dream* with no attempt at period costume. He applied this then-unusual principle to his own production of *Hamlet*, which he dressed and set in his own time of the immediate post-war. Among the enthusiastic reviews was a comment that it was a 'perfect expression of a shell-shocked world'. The court wore evening dress, Ophelia danced the Charleston and, at the core of the play, Hamlet was 'the gloomy Dane with a cigarette'.

This production fuelled the discussion, which continues today, about 'updating' Shakespeare. Various arguments are put forward, both for and against:

- Wearing contemporary dress is simply reverting to an old tradition: Shakespeare's actors wore the costume of 1600; David Garrick's actors wore the powdered wigs and frock coats of the mid 18th century. It was the 19th century that engaged in historical research.

- Shakespeare's plays are written in the language, traditions and beliefs of his period. These are eroded if the costume that helps to express them is abandoned.

- It is inconsistent to demand that Shakespeare's exact words be spoken, but then to permit great freedom in choice of costume.

- It is a distraction to ask an audience to think about Shakespeare's 1600; to interpret the play for one's own period is the sole aim of any production.

- The plays may be set in any period of history if that period helps to convey their genuine issues and themes.

- The proper way to design and dress Shakespeare's plays is to create a style that suggests no particular period.

- An eclectic style is best: a designer should feel free to mix costumes from different periods.

- It is easier to be timeless and symbolic in set design than in costumes; what people wear cannot avoid being specific to time and place.

- Timelessness suits the tragedies because their meaning is universal and unchanging; comedies are based in the social life of a particular period.

▶ Which of the above points of view do you find to be strong arguments, and which weak?

▶ Apply these arguments about period and modern costume to any Shakespeare plays that you know.

▶ Design three or four costumes for a Shakespeare play, not in the dress of its original performance, but in today's modern dress. Explain your decisions about style, colour, textures, fabrics, etc. in terms of the characters who will wear them.

The text: tampering with Shakespeare's language

It is often said that Shakespeare's language is the core of his work – not his stories, characters or spectacular moments. Therefore, it is argued, the language should remain unaltered. The director is then free to be creative with period, set, costume, lighting, sound effects, type of theatre, etc. This view is largely based on the universal praise for Shakespeare as a great poet, and poetry has often been judged a purer and nobler art than play-writing (see Part 2, page 50). We would be less inclined to alter a poem and then offer it as the original poet's work. After 1800, there was also a growing desire to move away from the drastic adaptations of Shakespeare's plays and to return to what he actually wrote.

There are several arguments against this view of Shakespeare's language:

- Theatre is above all a visual art. If the freedom to re-create all the visual aspects of a play is accepted, it is illogical to single out language as being sacrosanct.

- Establishing precisely what Shakespeare wrote is difficult in many cases and impossible in some. Many editors have spent countless hours attempting it (see Part 1, page 41). It is fruitless to insist on fidelity to Shakespeare's text if one can't be sure what that text was.

- Since Shakespeare was very ready to adapt other playwrights' work (and frequent revision was common practice in his day), why should we be so scrupulous with his words?

- The nature and reception of Shakespeare's plays are bound to alter as audiences alter with different generations. Since every production will be something new, it is better described as a play 'based on what Shakespeare wrote'.

- Shakespeare has been 'used' for operas like Benjamin Britten's *A Midsummer Night's Dream*, for musicals like *West Side Story* (based on *Romeo and Juliet*) and for any number of films. If one is prepared to alter his language so radically in these media, why should anyone be criticised for altering it less when presenting a slightly doctored theatre production of the play?

- Much of Shakespeare's language is archaic and obscure. This is a particular problem in the creative wit and banter of the comedies. Audiences enjoy these plays for their lively stories, colour, romance and characters. Characters like Benedick, Beatrice, Falstaff, Rosalind and most of the clowns exist not in the elevated world of heroism but in the lively muddle of the 'real' world. It is unreasonable to perpetuate a language barrier that reduces this enjoyment.

▶ Which of the views expressed above do you most (and least) agree with?

An example of 'tampering' with Shakespeare's language occurred when the poet Robert Graves was commissioned to adapt *Much Ado About Nothing* for a 1965 production at The National Theatre by Franco Zefirelli, then a leading theatre and film director of Shakespeare. Graves rewrote some of the comic dialogue spoken by and about Beatrice and Benedick. Here is an example of Benedick's words from Act 1 when he extricates himself from his friends' mockery:

Shakespeare	Graves
Nay, mock not, mock not: the body of your discourse is sometime guarded with fragments, and the guards are but slightly basted on, neither; ere you flout old ends any further, examine your conscience: and so I leave you.	Nay, mock not, mock not. The body of your discourse is faced with bright patches of fancy and they none too closely stitched on neither. Ere you flout sober custom further, examine your consciences; and so I leave you.

▶ Using the notes and glossary of your edition, try rewriting a complicated or obscure passage of Shakespeare to make it more accessible. A colleague does the same for another page. Exchange your new versions, compare them with the original and discuss what may have been lost in the process.

Cutting the text for performance

Perhaps the strongest argument for not playing precisely what Shakespeare wrote comes when one considers the practice of cutting the text. Virtually all companies remove lines for performance. This is not rewriting Shakespeare, but it *is* still a form of alteration. Reasons for cutting include:

- Long plays like *Richard III, Cymbeline* and *Hamlet* run for nearly five hours if uncut. Audiences need to catch their last bus or train to get home. The director Trevor Nunn commented: 'When you approach the text of *Hamlet* the cutting virtually is the production.' Over 1000 lines could be cut. Depending on the directors' choices, one *Hamlet* could be a very different piece of writing from another.

- Sometimes (and this is a practice often condemned) directors cut sections of the play because they contradict a preconceived view of what the director wants to convey. For example, a heroic version of *Henry V* may remove sections like the cynical discussion about war-motives in Act 1, the slaughter of the French prisoners and the execution of the king's old friend Bardolph, because these episodes may well damage a view of Henry as the noblest English king.

- Obscure language (see page 73, above) is more likely to be cut than rewritten. However, Peter Hall declares that he cuts these days far less than he did when he first started directing. He argues that, if the audience doesn't understand, it is the actor, not Shakespeare, who is likely to be at fault. It is the director's job to help the actor to express unfamiliar or heightened language so that it communicates vividly.

▶ Which course should prevail: retaining what Shakespeare wrote, or altering it to help the director to deliver a clear message?

The playwright Tom Stoppard has had some mischievous fun with the practice of cutting text. In addition to writing *Rosencrantz and Guildenstern Are Dead* (1967), in which the action of *Hamlet* is seen from the point of view of two minor courtiers, he wrote a 15-minute *Hamlet* (1979) which ends with a farcical encore in which the whole play is reduced to three minutes. Only Shakespeare's words are used.

▶ Compare a Shakespeare play with a film or musical adaptation of it (e.g. *Romeo and Juliet* with the Baz Luhrman film or *West Side Story*). What do you think are the advantages and disadvantages of the new treatment? Can an adaptation be faithful to the spirit, if not to the text, of a play?

Psychoanalytic approaches

In the 20th century psychoanalysis became a major influence on the understanding and interpretation of human behaviour. The founder of psychoanalysis, Sigmund Freud (1856–1939), explained personality as the result of unconscious and irrational desires, repressed memories or wishes, sexuality, fantasy, anxiety and conflict. Freud's theories have had strong influence on criticism and on the staging of Shakespeare's plays, especially the tragedies, which dramatise violent and erratic behaviour.

Macbeth has been an obvious play for post-Freudian investigation. In fact, Freud himself wrote a brief study on Lady Macbeth, speculating on the couple's childless state. In her first scene she summons the powers of darkness to 'unsex' her so that she can achieve a ruthless resolve; she has to support her husband when tension makes him erratic; she has to play the role of gracious queen; and finally she has to deal with rejection when Macbeth retreats into the darkness of his own mind. The result is despair, breakdown and suicide. But the role as written has very few lines to support this mental journey and its huge significance in the play. Several actresses have felt the need to create 'back-stories', such as Freud might have drawn from a real-life Lady Macbeth on his psychiatrist's couch. What were her relations with her father (whom she mentions while Macbeth is murdering Duncan)? Did she have a child that died? And, within the play, what are the details of her life between the banquet and the sleepwalking scene in Act 4? She undergoes a horrifying change but Shakespeare shows none of its process.

Characters in other plays also seem to invite Freudian analysis:

- Is Juliet isolated, enclosed, unloved and needing to escape from a domineering (older) father and cold (younger) mother?

- What of King Lear's marriage? There is no mention of a wife. Has he been in emotional solitude and become addicted to robust, noisy male company so that he has no idea of how to make real contact with his daughters?

- What are Hamlet's underlying feelings about his dead father and living mother? Freud's concept of the Oedipus complex suggests that subconsciously Hamlet had sexual feelings for his mother and wanted to replace his father.

If directors and actors discuss, improvise and rehearse these back-stories, the results in performance will generally be subtle and implicit. In stage performances it is rare actually to illustrate such scenes which Shakespeare didn't write (but see below, page 81). They are more likely to be explored on film than on stage. However, some scenes (e.g. Hamlet's visit to his mother's bedroom or Old Capulet's bullying Juliet into marrying Paris) force directors and actors to consider the characters' subconscious, as well as their conscious, motivations.

Of all Shakespeare's plays, *Measure for Measure* provides the most fruitful ground for psychoanalytic interpretation. A crucial line is Angelo's 'We are all frail' in Act 2 when he is struggling with his feelings for Isabella, the novice nun. Different types of frailty afflict almost all the characters, but most strikingly those who set themselves the highest moral standards. The Duke of Vienna abandons his authority, then takes the disguise of a friar to investigate the city which seems to be falling into promiscuous chaos. Early 20th-century productions would present him as wise, controlled and humane; nowadays audiences are more likely to see a neurotic, inadequate Duke. But the play's most intense drama centres on Angelo and Isabella: he prides himself on utter self-control and rectitude; she wants strict discipline in a convent. Before Freud, productions would present Isabella's virtue as admirable; now she is more likely to be a victim of anxiety, running away from disturbing truths hidden in her psyche.

In 1973 Jonathan Miller directed a low-budget production of the play for The National Theatre at The Old Vic. Setting it in the Vienna of the 1930s, he implicitly wanted the audience to think of Freud (who came from Vienna) and to consider the dangers of sexual repression. The staging was based on a long corridor with cells leading off. This could suggest a claustrophobic tension and locked-up areas of the mind. Its drab office ambience implied that bureaucratic efficiency could be a refuge for frail personalities.

Reviews were mixed. One reviewer thought that modern dress (or dress of the 1920s and 1930s) was bound to mute the play's eloquence and work against the often-elevated language. Another found the calculated skill of mood and movement similar to qualities in a Pinter production. But there was much consternation about Miller's treatment of Shakespeare's ending. Generally, productions had interpreted Isabella's silence as decorous acceptance of the Duke's marriage proposal. Miller had her shrink away in horror, as though the Duke were another Angelo, sexually threatening and thus leading to a repeat of her crisis of Act 2. Michael Billington, in his review (the *Guardian*, 10 November 1973), gave three objections, the first more precise than the other two:

> ... it's an ending inadequately prepared for by the two performers, unsanctioned by Shakespeare, and, I'd say, offensive to those who respect the original.

Since 1973, directors have read all sorts of possibilities into Isabella's silence, more of them disturbing than life-affirming. (See extract in Part 4, page 98.)

▶ Reread the section 'Character or stereotype?' (Part 1, page 19). How far removed is this post-Freudian treatment of Shakespeare from the way the plays were presented to audiences of 1600?

Feminist approaches

Feminism has had a considerable impact on the ways in which Shakespeare can now be presented. It has protested against the 'male ownership' of interpretation. Until very recently most critics and all directors of Shakespeare were men; men decided which questions should be asked of the plays and which answers were acceptable. This maleness could neglect, distort or patronise the female point of view.

Feminists challenge sexism: those beliefs and practices that result in the oppression and subordination of women. Feminism reveals how gender roles are shaped to the disadvantage of women in family, work, politics and religion. It exposes the male prejudices which for millennia have portrayed women as inferior.

Many of Shakespeare's comedies show resourceful, mature women managing to defy the limitations of a patriarchy (a male-dominated society). In *As You Like It*, Rosalind is seen to educate Orlando into recognising his potential for a fuller emotional life. In *The Merchant of Venice*, Portia rescues Antonio and the state of law in Venice whilst promoting the values of (female) mercy above (male) justice.

In tragedy traditionally male values are generally even more entrenched. Tragedies (and history plays) deal with politics, revenge, battles and family dynasties – all these are male territory. When virtuous, women often play stereotypical roles: dutiful daughter, submissive bride, gracious hostess, mother to the noble heir. Rebellious or divergent behaviour in women can cast them into an opposite stereotype: Othello accuses Desdemona of being a whore; in *King Lear* Goneril and Regan become cruel and murderous; Lady Macbeth, who prays to be made unnatural ('unsex me here'), eventually breaks down and commits suicide. For women in these plays there seems to be little in between the extremes of virtue and vice.

It is therefore refreshing to listen to Emilia in Act 4 of *Othello*. Her role has gathered importance in 20th-century productions and she speaks what is virtually a feminist manifesto:

> Let husbands know
> Their wives have sense like them: they see, and smell,
> And have their palates both for sweet and sour
> As husbands have. What is it that they do
> When they change us for others? Is it sport?
> I think it is. And doth affection breed it?
> I think it doth. Is't frailty that thus errs?
> It is so too. And have not we affections,
> Desires for sport, and frailty, as men have?
> Then let them use us well; else let them know
> The ills we do, their ills instruct us so.

Emilia is speaking to her mistress Desdemona, who has been cruelly treated by her husband, but whose upbringing and beliefs are more conventional, so that she is more ready to excuse men's behaviour. This scene has given scope for varied interpretation. Does an audience admire both women equally but for different reasons? Does Emilia speak with angry indignation, or with wise tolerance?

Feminist approaches have influenced many productions in the late 20th century and have revealed new possibilities in several of the plays:

- In *The Taming of the Shrew*, Katherine is not necessarily tamed into compliance with men. Her final speech, urging submission, has been played ironically to mean the opposite. In some productions, she has been so utterly broken that the play becomes a protest against male inhumanity. In others, she has tamed Petruchio so that he is ready to become a feminist spokesman.

- In *Hamlet*, Ophelia's decline into madness can be very different from 19th-century sentimentalism and can become an uncomfortable protest against the ways in which men (Polonius, Laertes, Hamlet, Claudius) have pursued their self-centred agendas.

- A feminist production of *Macbeth* saw the Witches as the real heroines. They were colourful, charismatic survivors, free from male restraints. If a production brings them on at the end, it can suggest that because their predictions are fulfilled they have scored an ironic triumph over men. The male future is in the hands of these despised female outcasts.

- A production of *A Midsummer Night's Dream* in 1986 saw the play as an exposure of male brutality. A reviewer picked on some incidents that surprised him: 'Egeus enters carrying a screaming Hermia over his shoulder, drops her on the floor like a sack of coal, and puts a knife to her throat … Theseus's hunting party pursues not a fox or rabbit or deer but Hippolyta herself.'

Political approaches

Shakespeare's plays can't help being about politics: they dramatise how people live together, how society is organised, where power lies, the conflicts that develop, if and how these conflicts are resolved. Critics differ on whether or not Shakespeare declared his own political beliefs.

- A traditional view sees him supporting the established hierarchy, with power in the hands of the monarch, the aristocracy and always with men rather than women.

- Other critics feel that he is subversive, showing authority as corrupt and misguided, and supporting malcontents like Edmund in *King Lear*. Some

Eastern European productions have staged *Hamlet* to show how a vicious surveillance society is challenged by a young prince whose principles are ahead of his time and who dies because the people are not yet ready to rise in rebellion.

- Some argue that Shakespeare doesn't take sides. His plays dramatise the complexities in society; they raise questions for audiences to debate and answer in their different ways.

Since Shakespeare's day, directors and actors have staged his plays to support various political views, chiefly, but not always, the traditional and conservative. Modern audiences may instinctively deplore this practice, but it can be justified: not only did Shakespeare live in an age before liberal views about tolerance and democracy took hold, he was also very ready to distort the stories and values of earlier times (e.g. ancient Rome, pre-Tudor England) to inform the political context of 1600.

More recent productions, particularly of Shakespeare's tragedies and histories, have sought to challenge traditional views of authority and established government. Many of these interpretations derive from the political theorist Karl Marx (1818–1883) and from Bertolt Brecht, the German playwright and director.

Brecht (1898–1956) developed an 'epic' theatre that aimed to promote left-wing social and political views, to abandon naturalism and theatrical illusion and to make the theatre a forum for intelligent debate. His own views and plays led other directors to apply these theories to Shakespeare, especially those plays that are most direct about social issues, such as *Julius Caesar* and *Coriolanus*. It is argued that plays like these can be seen as fables: they tell stories about distant times and places as ways of making audiences consider contemporary issues like dictatorship, democracy and equality.

In 2007, as part of The Royal Shakespeare Company's season of Complete Works, the Berliner Ensemble (the company that Brecht himself had founded in 1949) brought their *Richard II* to Stratford. This play is one of Shakespeare's early histories, full of sensitive poetry which explores the king's view of his own semi-divine royalty and his self-regard as he is overthrown by his pragmatic cousin Bullingbrook (Bolingbroke). This production was harsh and arresting, its design of set and costume an austere black and white, which could also convey a superficial elegance. The ruling classes (i.e. virtually all the characters) were grasping egotists, some on the very edge of sanity, suggesting that power lies in the hands of monstrous children who are destroying their inheritance. There was some relief in the grim comedy, emphasised by actors' white faces, which turned rulers into malevolent jesters. As Richard lost control, the pure white screens of the set were streaked with filth. Shakespeare describes the king's journey through the city with Londoners turning against him; in this production the offstage crowd hurled lumps of mud against the screens so that the stage filled with rubbish and water. Beneath any detailed political messages, the production was based on a very brutish view of human nature.

The 20th century contained times of unspeakable brutality, such as the regimes of Stalin, Hitler and Idi Amin of Uganda, and repressive philosophies like that of apartheid in South Africa. It also became a century of struggle towards finer values: democracy, tolerance and respect for the individual. That continued, most memorably in 2007 with the commemoration of the 200th anniversary of the abolition of the slave trade. How, therefore, can today's Shakespeare productions deal with *Othello* and Shylock in *The Merchant of Venice*? Many plays dramatise the position of outsiders, but Shylock and the Moor have become especially sensitive cases in the last 50 years.

In the London of 1600 prejudices against 'blackamoors' included some that will sound depressingly familiar today: they are sexual predators; they will easily revert to barbarism; foreign immigrants should be transported. In *Titus Andronicus* Shakespeare made the blackness of Aaron, the Moor, synonymous with his vicious amorality; in *The Merchant of Venice*, Portia, the heroine, contemptuously dismisses Morocco, her first suitor, 'Let all of his complexion choose me so.' How can Shakespeare, the wise and humane playwright, casually support such damaging prejudice? We are led to ask this question because for us racial prejudice eclipses all other types of discrimination. A contemporary director is thus likely to approach Shylock and Othello with particular anxieties.

In some ways Othello is more difficult because he is the focus of the play. Though it is not a huge part, every other character is drawn by his charisma: they think and talk about him constantly. He is a celebrated military leader in sophisticated Venetian society, he marries a beautiful white girl against her father's wishes, he offends his long-serving sergeant-major by appointing an inexperienced young officer above him. He then sacks his new officer for drunkenness. He is tricked into believing his wife has committed adultery and descends into jealousy so damaging that it drives him to the brink of madness. Eventually he murders his wife and commits suicide.

Everything about Othello is extreme: his nobility, his misjudgements, his passions. Shakespeare is not inhibited by any sense of political correctness in presenting racial issues, and so he is able to be creatively bold but politically elusive. It is possible for a modern director to let the play either support mixed marriages or warn against them; Othello himself may be either supremely dignified or a savage wearing the thinnest veneer of civilisation.

Deconstruction

In literary criticism 'deconstruction' can have several different but related meanings. If a stage production is considered as a type of critical interpretation of the play, then deconstruction (or 'postmodernism', as it is often called) will refer to a mixture of styles. The director and his or her company will reject a single coherent interpretation as too conventional and oversimplifying. They may feel that the play's richness can be found not by selecting a single approach, but by welcoming anomalies and risking confusion to highlight the play's perceived underlying lack of a consistent vision. They may:

- choose costumes and weapons from different historical periods

- fragment a speech and share the lines among various speakers

- break up a named character's part and have different actors each play an aspect of the personality

- use the language (or some of it) as a springboard for dance and varieties of physical and circus-style performing.

When a company adopts these approaches they generally do so with energy, a spirit of carnival and a risk-taking desire to experiment. Audiences may then be invited not to see a finished product but to share the 'work in progress', accepting that all remains in flux, and that the next night's performance may have moved on to a different stage of the experiment.

At the end of his introduction to the Oxford Shakespeare edition of *The Tempest* (see Part 6, page 121), Stephen Orgel refers to Peter Brook's 1968 production at The Roundhouse:

> Brook's production was ... designed to explore and release the play's ambivalent, disruptive and frankly violent energies. What resulted, in the words of Margaret Croydon, 'was not a literal interpretation of Shakespeare's play but a working out of abstractions, essences and contradictions embedded in the text. The plot was shattered, condensed, deverbalised; time was continuous, shifting ...'. Not surprisingly, the energy thereby released was primarily sexual and rebellious, the energy most feared and most suppressed in the text. Ferdinand and Miranda meet and make love, parodied by Ariel and Caliban, and subsequently by other members of the cast. Prospero undertakes to train and subjugate Caliban by teaching him to speak: the vocabulary consists of 'I', 'you', 'food', 'love', 'master', 'slave'. But the last two words release Caliban's rebelliousness and his libido; he escapes from Prospero, accomplishes the rape of Miranda, and takes over the island.

▶ How, on the basis of this description of the Roundhouse production, can Peter Brook be said to have deconstructed *The Tempest*?

The director Charles Marowitz, who had worked with Peter Brook, was equally free in deconstructing Shakespeare's texts. When he adapted *Macbeth* and *The Taming of the Shrew*, he broke up the plays and rearranged their fragments into types of collage which were intended to be subversive, especially to audiences who knew the accepted versions. This approach can be compared to late 17th-century adaptations (see Part 2, page 44). However, Marowitz turned those principles upside down. The neo-classical authors had wanted to impose order upon the irregular Shakespeare: Marowitz aimed to dis-order plays which he thought had become too settled and traditional.

4 | Extracts and performance issues

The following extracts are listed in chronological order of each play's composition. The questions that follow the extracts are designed to raise issues about interpretation through performance. They should be investigated in the light both of the historical evolution of Shakespeare production from 1600 to the present time (as outlined in Parts 1 and 2) and of the critical approaches discussed in Part 3.

From *The Two Gentlemen of Verona*

Proteus has travelled from Verona to Milan to follow his friend Valentine who is serving the Duke. Valentine and the Duke's daughter Silvia have secretly fallen in love, though the Duke intends that his friend Sir Turio will marry Silvia. When Proteus sees Silvia he becomes obsessed with her and treacherously betrays Valentine, who is then banished by the Duke. Proteus then offers to help Turio in his suit, and (in this extract) joins him in an evening serenade outside Silvia's window. Unknown to any of these characters, Proteus's girl-friend Julia has followed him from Verona and, with the landlord of the local pub, watches the process of his double treachery.

TURIO	How now, Sir Proteus, are you crept before us?	
PROTEUS	Ay, gentle Turio, for you know that love	
	Will creep in service where it cannot go.	
TURIO	Ay, but I hope, sir, that you love not here.	
PROTEUS	Sir, but I do; or else I would be hence.	5
TURIO	Who? Silvia?	
PROTEUS	Ay, Silvia, for your sake.	
TURIO	I thank you for your own. Now, gentlemen,	
	Let's tune, and to it lustily awhile.	

[*Enter* HOST *and* JULIA *disguised as page*]

HOST	Now, my young guest, methinks you're allycholly. I pray you, why is it?	10
JULIA	Marry, mine host, because I cannot be merry.	
HOST	Come, we'll have you merry; I'll bring you where you shall hear music and see the gentleman that you asked for.	
JULIA	But shall I hear him speak?	
HOST	Ay, that you shall.	15
JULIA	That will be music!	

[Prelude to the song begins]

HOST	Hark! Hark!
JULIA	Is he among these?
HOST	Ay; but peace, let's hear 'em.

Song

Who is Silvia? What is she,   20
    That all our swains commend her?
Holy, fair and wise is she;
    The heaven such grace did lend her
That she might admirèd be.

Is she kind as she is fair?   25
    For Beauty lives with Kindness.
Love doth to her eyes repair
    To help him of his blindness,
And, being helped, inhabits there.

Then to Silvia let us sing   30
    That Silvia is excelling;
She excels each mortal thing
    Upon the dull earth dwelling.
To her let us garlands bring.

HOST	How now, are you sadder than you were before? How do 35 you, man? The music likes you not.
JULIA	You mistake; the musician likes me not.
HOST	Why, my pretty youth?
JULIA	He plays false, father.
HOST	How, out of tune on the strings? 40
JULIA	Not so; but yet so false that he grieves my very heart-strings.
HOST	You have a quick ear.
JULIA	Ay, I would I were deaf; it makes me have a slow heart.
HOST	I perceive you delight not in music.
JULIA	Not a whit when it jars so.

(Act 4 Scene 2: lines 18–62)

Performance issues

1 Double action: There are layers of deceit and **irony** in this extract. Proteus is
confidently tricking Turio (who even raises the question of love-rivalry). But he
is watched and judged by Julia in disguise and at a distance. The Host, who is
with her, thinks she is a boy made melancholy by soulful music. As audience we
watch both layers of action and understand all levels of deceit. A director has to

decide on the atmosphere and staging of this 'play-within-a-play'. Moods range between suffering and light comedy. How may the actors express these?

2 Music: This is one of Shakespeare's most beautiful and famous songs. There is also some witty and punning talk about the techniques and effects of music. Does this encourage comedy?

3 Who sings the song? Is it a professional singer? Is it Turio – who has written the song? Is it Proteus – who wants to be noticed by Silvia? Some productions have included attendants and even a supporting choir. Would you make this a grand moment or is it better limited to the four characters?

4 The song occupies some time. What does Julia do while this happens?

From *Titus Andronicus*

Titus, a successful Roman general, has been brutally treated by the emperor and the emperor's new wife Tamora. Her sons have raped Titus' daughter Lavinia and cut off her tongue and hands; then, in trying to save his own sons from execution, Titus has cut off his hand as proof of obedience. Here a messenger tells him that his sacrifice has been mocked. He faces his disasters with his family around him: Lavinia, his brother Marcus, and his eldest son Lucius.

MESSENGER	Worthy Andronicus, ill art thou repaid	
	For that good hand thou sent'st the emperor.	
	Here are the heads of thy two noble sons	
	And here's thy hand in scorn to thee sent back:	
	Thy grief their sports, thy resolution mocked,	5
	That woe is me to think upon thy woes,	
	More than remembrance of my father's death. *Exit*	
MARCUS	Now let hot Etna cool in Sicily	
	And be my heart an ever-burning hell!	
	These miseries are more than may be borne.	10
	To weep with them that weep doth ease some deal	
	But sorrow flouted at is double death.	
LUCIUS	Ah, that this sight should make so deep a wound,	
	And yet detested life not shrink thereat!	
	That ever death should let life bear his name,	15
	Where life hath no more interest but to breathe!	

[*Lavinia kisses Titus*]

MARCUS	Alas poor heart, that kiss is comfortless	
	As frozen water to a starvèd snake.	
TITUS	When will this fearful slumber have an end?	
MARCUS	Now farewell flatt'ry; die Andronicus,	20

                Thou dost not slumber: see thy two sons' heads,
                Thy warlike hand, thy mangled daughter here,
                Thy other banished son with this dear sight
                Struck pale and bloodless, and thy brother, I,
                Even like a stony image, cold and numb.   25
                Ah, now no more will I control thy griefs;
                Rent off thy silver hair, thy other hand
                Gnawing with thy teeth, and be this dismal sight
                The closing up of our most wretched eyes.
                Now is a time to storm; why art thou still?   30
TITUS   Ha ha ha!
MARCUS   Why dost thou laugh? It fits not with this hour.
TITUS   Why, I have not another tear to shed;
                Besides, this sorrow is an enemy,
                And would usurp upon my wat'ry eyes   35
                And make them blind with tributary tears.
                Then which way shall I find Revenge's cave?
                For these two heads do seem to speak to me
                And threat me I shall never come to bliss
                Till all these mischiefs be returned again,   40
                Even in their throats that hath committed them.
                Come, let me see what task I have to do;
                You heavy people, circle me about
                That I may turn me to each one of you
                And swear upon my soul to right your wrongs.   45
                The vow is made. Come, brother, take a head,
                And in this hand the other will I bear;
                And Lavinia, thou shalt be employed in these arms;
                Bear thou my hand, sweet wench, between thy teeth.
                As for thee, boy, go get thee from my sight;   50
                Thou art an exile, and thou must not stay;
                Hie to the Goths and raise an army there;
                And if ye love me, as I think you do,
                Let's kiss and part, for we have much to do.

                                        Exeunt [all but Lucius]
                                        (Act 3 Scene 1: lines 233–286)

Performance issues

1   The play's dramatic interest centres increasingly on the family group. A
    director has to consider how private individuals and their relationships can be
    seen within the context of public Roman values. For example, ancient Rome
    is generally dominated by men and their achievements. Here the mutilated

Lavinia has been the focus of Act 3; the men in her family have to come to terms with her violation. How is this different from avenging a wrong done to a man? Remember too that she speaks no more words in the play; she now has no tongue to speak of her grief and loss.

2   There are moments in this scene when characters seem to acknowledge that suffering has gone far beyond the power of words to express it. How might this affect the words they *do* find? For example, should the rhetoric be declamatory or muted?

3   Comedy: It may seem odd even to think of comedy in a play so full of horrors, but some types of laughter may contribute to a tragedy, whilst others should be avoided. Here, for example, Titus laughs (line 31) and surprises his conventional brother Marcus. Their exit is even more extraordinary: Titus orders Lavinia, whose own hands have been lopped off, to carry his hand in her clenched teeth.

4   Ritual: Titus dismisses tears as an improper response because he needs to be clear-eyed and clear-headed to fulfil his duty of revenge. He elevates revenge into a sacred duty, which his family must share: 'You heavy people, circle me about'. How might this moment be staged and how can it lead into the strange manner of their exit?

5   In Act 4 Lucius' young son will appear, replacing his father, who by then has been banished from Rome. Some productions include him in this earlier scene too. Do you find any dramatic point in having a child witness these extremes of suffering?

From *A Midsummer Night's Dream*

This is the sleeping part of the play. The four lovers, driven frantic by the love-juice and the confusion of the dark night, have all been brought separately and exhausted to the same area, where they have fallen asleep. Bottom, transformed into an ass, has been parted from his terrified fellow actors and has met Titania, the Queen of Fairies. She is delighted with him, entertains him as a specially favoured court guest, then falls asleep with him. Oberon watches them and begins to regret how he has humiliated his wife Titania.

OBERON   [*Coming forward.*]
Welcome, good Robin. Seest thou this sweet sight?
Her dotage now I do begin to pity;
For, meeting her of late behind the wood
Seeking sweet favours for this hateful fool,

I did upbraid her and fall out with her,   5
For she his hairy temples then had rounded
With coronet of fresh and fragrant flowers;
And that same dew, which sometime on the buds
Was wont to swell like round and orient pearls,
Stood now within the pretty flowerets' eyes   10
Like tears that did their own disgrace bewail.
When I had at my pleasure taunted her,
And she in mild terms begged my patience,
I then did ask of her her changeling child,
Which straight she gave me, and her fairy sent   15
To bear him to my bower in Fairyland.
And now I have the boy, I will undo
This hateful imperfection of her eyes.
And, gentle Puck, take this transformèd scalp
From off the head of this Athenian swain,   20
That, he awaking when the other do,
May all to Athens back again repair,
And think no more of this night's accidents
But as the fierce vexation of a dream.
But first I will release the Fairy Queen.   25

> [*Squeezing a herb on Titania's eyes.*]

Be as thou wast wont to be;
See as thou wast wont to see.
Dian's bud o'er Cupid's flower
Hath such force and blessèd power.
Now, my Titania, wake you, my sweet Queen!   30

TITANIA   [*Starting up.*]
My Oberon, what visions have I seen!
Methought I was enamoured of an ass.

OBERON   There lies your love.

TITANIA   How came these things to pass?
O, how mine eyes do loathe his visage now!

OBERON   Silence awhile: Robin, take off this head.   35
Titania, music call, and strike more dead
Than common sleep of all these five the sense.

TITANIA   Music, ho, music such as charmeth sleep!

> [*Soft music plays.*]

PUCK   [*To Bottom, removing the ass's head*]
Now when thou wak'st, with thine own fool's eyes peep.

OBERON   Sound, music! Come, my Queen, take hands with me,   40
And rock the ground whereon these sleepers be.

[They dance.]

Now thou and I are new in amity,
And will tomorrow midnight solemnly
Dance in Duke Theseus' house triumphantly,
And bless it to all fair prosperity.   45
There shall the pairs of faithful lovers be
Wedded, with Theseus, all in jollity.

PUCK   Fairy King, attend, and mark:
                I do hear the morning lark.

OBERON   Then, my Queen, in silence sad,   50
                Trip we after night's shade;
                We the globe can compass soon,
                Swifter than the wandering moon.

TITANIA   Come, my lord, and in our flight
                Tell me how it came this night   55
                That I sleeping here was found
                With these mortals on the ground.

Exeunt Oberon, Titania and Puck

Wind horns. Enter THESEUS *with* HIPPOLYTA, EGEUS, *and all his train.*

THESEUS   Go, one of you, find out the forester;
                For now our observation is performed,
                And since we have the vaward of the day,   60
                My love shall hear the music of my hounds.
                Uncouple in the western valley; let them go:
                Dispatch, I say, and find the forester.

(Act 4 Scene 1: lines 43–105)

Performance issues

1   Directors need to plan carefully how to place the sleepers around the stage.
    Eventually the hunting party will discover the four lovers, who must be
    unobtrusive during this extract. Bottom is entwined with Titania, but must not
    be noticed by the other mortals: he remains asleep until line 196. Consider how
    these different parts of the action could be managed on various types of stage
    (e.g. the 1600 Globe, in a proscenium theatre, in a small studio space).

2   Some productions use a single actor to double Oberon and Theseus, and
    another (male or female) for Titania and Hippolyta. This device can bring
    benefits and disadvantages for the play as a whole; these need to be discussed
    beyond this Act 4 moment. Here there is a practical difficulty of how to change
    actors from fairy royalty to mortal, hunting royalty. Is it better to conceal the
    change or make some strong theatrical effect from it?

3   *A Midsummer Night's Dream* contains a great deal of music. Directors need to
find a coherent style for it, but also to notice the very different purposes when
it is used. In this extract you need to consider the dance for Oberon and Titania,
the 'musical confusion' that Theseus orders, possibly some sound effect for the
love juice, and perhaps another effect for dawn appearing.

4   Is this extract devoted wholly to dignified reconciliation? If there are other
strands that contrast, or even clash, consider what weight to give them. Puck's
mockery? Titania's horror? Bottom's appearance? And some productions find a
continuing tension in the relationship of Theseus and Hippolyta.

5   What can 'dream' in the title mean? Productions have ranged between the
extremes of sentimental beauty and ghastly nightmare. You may find Oberon's
lines helpful:

> And think no more of this night's accidents
> But as the fierce vexation of a dream.

From *King Richard III*

This play continues the story of the Wars of the Roses, dramatised in preceding
plays, the three parts of *Henry VI*. Richard of Gloucester, not yet King Richard
III, is one of the Yorkist brothers; another has achieved the crown as Edward IV;
another is George, Duke of Clarence, who appears at the end of this extract on his
way to prison. Richard is responsible for the intrigues that have put Clarence in
grave danger. Shakespeare opens the play with Richard's soliloquy, celebrating the
success of the House of York and showing how he intends to use this 'piping time
of peace'.

Enter RICHARD DUKE OF GLOUCESTER

RICHARD   Now is the winter of our discontent
Made glorious summer by this son of York,
And all the clouds that loured upon our house
In the deep bosom of the ocean buried.
Now are our brows bound with victorious wreaths,   5
Our bruisèd arms hung up for monuments,
Our stern alarums changed to merry meetings,
Our dreadful marches to delightful measures.
Grim-visaged war hath smoothed his wrinkled front,
And now, instead of mounting barbèd steeds   10
To fright the souls of fearful adversaries,
He capers nimbly in a lady's chamber
To the lascivious pleasing of a lute.

But I that am not shaped for sportive tricks
Nor made to court an amorous looking-glass,   15
I that am rudely stamped and want love's majesty
To strut before a wanton ambling nymph,
I that am curtailed of this fair proportion,
Cheated of feature by dissembling nature,
Deformed, unfinished, sent before my time   20
Into this breathing world scarce half made up,
And that so lamely and unfashionable
That dogs bark at me as I halt by them,
Why, I, in this weak piping time of peace,
Have no delight to pass away the time,   25
Unless to see my shadow in the sun
And descant on mine own deformity.
And therefore, since I cannot prove a lover
To entertain these fair well-spoken days,
I am determinèd to prove a villain   30
And hate the idle pleasures of these days.
Plots have I laid, inductions dangerous,
By drunken prophecies, libels, and dreams
To set my brother Clarence and the king
In deadly hate the one against the other.   35
And if King Edward be as true and just
As I am subtle, false, and treacherous,
This day should Clarence closely be mewed up
About a prophecy which says that 'G'
Of Edward's heirs the murderer shall be.   40
Dive, thoughts, down to my soul, here Clarence comes.

Enter CLARENCE *and* BRAKENBURY, *guarded*

Brother, good day. What means this armèd guard
That waits upon your grace?

CLARENCE   His majesty,
Tend'ring my person's safety, hath appointed
This conduct to convey me to the Tower.   45

RICHARD   Upon what cause?

CLARENCE   Because my name is George.

RICHARD   Alack, my lord, that fault is none of yours.
He should for that commit your godfathers.
Oh, belike his majesty hath some intent
That you should be new christened in the Tower.   50
But what's the matter, Clarence? May I know?

CLARENCE   Yea, Richard, when I know, but I protest
As yet I do not. But as I can learn,

He hearkens after prophecies and dreams,
And from the cross-row plucks the letter 'G',   55
And says a wizard told him that by 'G'
His issue disinherited should be.
And for my name of George begins with 'G',
It follows in his thought that I am he.
These, as I learn, and suchlike toys as these   60
Hath moved his highness to commit me now.

RICHARD   Why, this it is when men are ruled by women.
'Tis not the king that sends you to the Tower.
My lady Grey, his wife, Clarence, 'tis she
That tempts him to this harsh extremity.   65

(Act 1 Scene 1: lines 1–65)

Performance issues

1   Continuation or fresh start? This is a recurring question with history plays.
    Should the single play explain everything within itself? Some productions
    continue the stories of *Henry VI* by a sort of overlap or reference back.
    Sometimes Richard cradles a child, sometimes there are images of his
    murdered father, sometimes armed soldiers lurk in the shadows. Or should he
    be simply alone for the soliloquy?

2   Soliloquy (see Part 1, page 35): Remember that this is an early Shakespeare play
    and that Richard inherits the theatre tradition of the medieval Vice figure. How
    lively is the relationship with the audience? Should they deplore the ruthless
    attitudes, or enjoy Richard's vitality? How do you establish a balance between
    the two? In some productions there is much comic gesture and animated
    caricature. In others he broods menacingly.

3   When Clarence appears, Richard asks several questions. Does he genuinely need
    information or is he playing at being naïve? What seems to be the relationship
    between the two brothers?

4   It is important for directors and actors to understand something of the late
    medieval political world of these history plays. Does it seem here to be based
    on sound principles or on childish whims? Can people understand and guard
    against dangers? How might this opening – in stage design and character
    behaviour – indicate these dangers?

From *The Merchant of Venice*

The merchant Antonio has failed to pay his debt and Shylock, the Jew, has had him arrested. In court the Duke and the other Christians have found no way of persuading Shylock to show mercy. Portia, disguised as a young lawyer, with Nerissa as her clerk, is now conducting the trial. She appears to be supporting Shylock's claim to have his forfeiture, a pound of Antonio's flesh, which he has the right to cut from his victim's heart in open court.

ANTONIO	Commend me to your honourable wife.	
	Tell her the process of Antonio's end,	
	Say how I loved you, speak me fair in death,	
	And when the tale is told, bid her be judge	
	Whether Bassanio had not once a love.	5
	Repent but you that you shall lose your friend	
	And he repents not that he pays your debt.	
	For if the Jew do cut but deep enough	
	I'll pay it instantly with all my heart.	
BASSANIO	Antonio, I am married to a wife	10
	Which is as dear to me as life itself;	
	But life itself, my wife, and all the world,	
	Are not with me esteemed above thy life.	
	I would lose all, ay, sacrifice them all	
	Here to this devil, to deliver you.	15
PORTIA	Your wife would give you little thanks for that	
	If she were by to hear you make the offer.	
GRATIANO	I have a wife who I protest I love;	
	I would she were in heaven, so she could	
	Entreat some power to change this currish Jew.	20
NERISSA	'Tis well you offer it behind her back;	
	The wish would make else an unquiet house.	
SHYLOCK	These be the Christian husbands! I have a daughter:	
	Would any of the stock of Barabbas	
	Had been her husband, rather than a Christian!	25
	We trifle time; I pray thee pursue sentence.	
PORTIA	A pound of that same merchant's flesh is thine,	
	The court awards it, and the law doth give it.	
SHYLOCK	Most rightful judge!	
PORTIA	And you must cut this flesh from off his breast;	30
	The law allows it, and the court awards it.	
SHYLOCK	Most learned judge! A sentence: come, prepare.	
PORTIA	Tarry a little, there is something else.	
	This bond doth give thee here no jot of blood.	
	The words expressly are 'a pound of flesh'.	35

	Take then thy bond, take thou thy pound of flesh,	
	But in the cutting it, if thou dost shed	
	One drop of Christian blood, thy lands and goods	
	Are by the laws of Venice confiscate	
	Unto the state of Venice.	
GRATIANO	O upright judge!	40
	Mark, Jew – O learned judge!	
SHYLOCK	Is that the law?	
PORTIA	Thyself shall see the Act.	
	For as thou urgest justice, be assured	
	Thou shalt have justice more than thou desirest.	
GRATIANO	O learned judge! Mark, Jew: a learned judge.	45
SHYLOCK	I take this offer then. Pay the bond thrice	
	And let the Christian go.	
BASSIANO	Here is the money.	
PORTIA	Soft.	
	The Jew shall have all justice; soft, no haste;	
	He shall have nothing but the penalty.	50
GRATIANO	O Jew, an upright judge, a learned judge!	
PORTIA	Therefore prepare thee to cut off the flesh.	
	Shed thou no blood, nor cut thou less nor more	
	But just a pound of flesh. If thou tak'st more	
	Or less than a just pound, be it but so much	55
	As makes it light or heavy in the substance	
	Or the division of the twentieth part	
	Of one poor scruple – nay, if the scale do turn	
	But in the estimation of a hair,	
	Thou diest, and all thy goods are confiscate.	60

(Act 4 Scene 1: lines 269–328)

Performance issues

1 Where is the court? This is an issue both of design and interpretation. Is it in public, staged with all the grandeur of the wealthy Venetian state? Or is the case so bizarre and embarrassing that the authorities have had it tucked away in some small, insignificant courtroom to avoid publicity?

2 A trial is a formal confrontation. How might the scene be staged so that the group of Christians (desperate at this point in the scene) are separate from Shylock, who appears to be succeeding?

3 Consider variety within this formality. For example, how can you distinguish the different feelings and reactions of the Duke, Antonio, Bassanio and Gratiano, who are all on the same side?

4   The start of this extract marks a pause in the proceedings. Antonio prepares for death, while Bassanio and Gratiano say what they would give for his release. All three speakers refer to Portia and Nerissa, without knowing they are present in disguise. Is the mood helped by comedy at this stage? How would you play the three speeches and the two women's comments?

5   View of Shylock: What does Portia think of him and of the disaster she is about to bring down on him? Does the audience have sympathy for him, for example, when he mentions his daughter Jessica? Or would an audience side with Gratiano and his views?

6   The critical moment occurs when Portia says, 'Tarry a little' and stops Shylock from cutting Antonio's flesh. Note how formal her language has been just before this moment. How might this moment be staged? With energy or a still focus? How might Shylock approach Antonio? How will the others behave?

From *As You Like It*

Rosalind, disguised as the boy Ganymede, has fled to the forest with Celia, her close friend and cousin. Orlando, who fell in love with her after the wrestling contest in court, has also been banished. They meet after Orlando has been pinning love poems to trees. 'Ganymede' offers to play 'Rosalind' in volatile and unexpected moods to cure Orlando of his love-obsession. He agrees but only because 'I would be talking of her'. In this scene he has arrived late for their appointment. Celia, calling herself 'Aliena', watches and very occasionally participates.

ROSALIND	Come, woo me, woo me; for now I am in a holiday humour and like enough to consent. What would you say to me now and I were your very, very Rosalind?	
ORLANDO	I would kiss before I spoke.	
ROSALIND	Nay, you were better speak first, and when you were gravelled for lack of matter you might take occasion to kiss. Very good orators when they are out, they will spit, and for lovers, lacking – God warrant us – matter, the cleanliest shift is to kiss.	5
ORLANDO	How if the kiss be denied?	10
ROSALIND	Then she puts you to entreaty, and there begins new matter.	
ORLANDO	Who could be out, being before his beloved mistress?	
ROSALIND	Marry, that should you if I were your mistress, or I should think my honesty ranker than my wit.	15
ORLANDO	What, of my suit?	

ROSALIND	Not out of your apparel, and yet out of your suit. Am not I your Rosalind?
ORLANDO	I take some joy to say you are, because I would be talking of her.
ROSALIND	Well, in her person, I say I will not have you.
ORLANDO	Then, in mine own person, I die.
ROSALIND	No, faith, die by attorney. The poor world is almost six thousand years old and in all this time there was not any man died in his own person, videlicet, in a love-cause. Troilus had his brains dashed out with a Grecian club, yet he did what he could to die before, and he is one of the patterns of love; Leander, he would have lived many a fair year though Hero had turned nun, if it had not been for a hot midsummer night, for, good youth, he went but forth to wash him in the Hellespont and, being taken with the cramp, was drowned, and the foolish chroniclers of that age found it was Hero of Sestos. But these are all lies: men have died from time to time – and worms have eaten them – but not for love.
ORLANDO	I would not have my right Rosalind of this mind, for I protest her frown might kill me.
ROSALIND	By this hand, it will not kill a fly. But come, now I will be your Rosalind in a more coming-on disposition and, ask me what you will, I will grant it.
ORLANDO	Then love me, Rosalind.
ROSALIND	Yes, faith, will I, Fridays and Saturdays and all.
ORLANDO	And wilt thou have me?
ROSALIND	Aye, and twenty such.
ORLANDO	What sayest thou?
ROSALIND	Are you not good?
ORLANDO	I hope so.
ROSALIND	Why then, can one desire too much of a good thing? – Come, sister, you shall be the priest and marry us. – Give me your hand, Orlando. – What do you say, sister?
ORLANDO	Pray thee marry us.
CELIA	I cannot say the words.
ROSALIND	You must begin: 'Will you, Orlando – '
CELIA	Go to. – Will you, Orlando, have to wife this Rosalind?
ORLANDO	I will.
ROSALIND	Aye, but when?
ORLANDO	Why, now, as fast as she can marry us.
ROSALIND	Then you must say, 'I take thee, Rosalind, for wife.'
ORLANDO	I take thee, Rosalind, for wife.
ROSALIND	I might ask you for your commission, but I do take thee,

20

25

30

35

40

45

50

55

60

	Orlando, for my husband. There's a girl goes before the
	priest, and certainly a woman's thought runs before her
	actions.
ORLANDO	So do all thoughts: they are winged.
ROSALIND	Now, tell me how long you would have her after you have
	possessed her?
ORLANDO	For ever and a day.
ROSALIND	Say a day without the 'ever'. No, no, Orlando: men are

ROSALIND   Now, tell me how long you would have her after you have   65
           possessed her?
ORLANDO   For ever and a day.
ROSALIND   Say a day without the 'ever'. No, no, Orlando: men are
           April when they woo, December when they wed; maids
           are May when they are maids, but the sky changes when   70
           they are wives. I will be more jealous of thee than a
           Barbary cock-pigeon over his hen; more clamorous than
           a parrot against rain, more new-fangled than an ape;
           more giddy in my desires than a monkey. I will weep for
           nothing, like Diana in the fountain, and I will do that   75
           when you are disposed to be merry. I will laugh like a
           hyena, and that when thou art inclined to sleep.

(Act 4 Scene 1: lines 55–125)

Performance issues

1   The forest: Traditional productions of *As You Like It* present either a 'real' forest
    (easiest to achieve in an open-air production) or a fairy-tale idealised version,
    perhaps more appropriate to the literary fiction of pastoral poetry. Some more
    recent productions have dispensed with scenery and relied on suggestive
    lighting; others, observing the artifice of this sophisticated play, have designed
    the location in freely abstract fashion, as though the forest is more a state of
    mind than a recognisable place.

2   Complicated games: Never in Shakespeare was the word 'play' more apt, and
    never did he attempt anything else so full of dizzying potential in terms of
    gender and role playing. When does Orlando recognise that he is with Rosalind
    rather than Ganymede? Some productions delay it until Rosalind appears as
    herself in Act 5. Some have him sense it before this scene begins. Others have
    located the moment at her line 58 in this scene, to which he replies, 'I take thee,
    Rosalind, for wife.'

3   Gender: Should women be cast in *As You Like It*? From 1660 to 1960 critics
    have delighted in star performances of Rosalind's femininity, especially when
    the actress can barely contain it beneath the boyish role of Ganymede. But
    maybe the playfulness flourishes most interestingly and authentically when
    all the players are men. At the heart of the playing is the accomplished boy

actor who plays Rosalind, who assumes the role of precocious Ganymede, who then pretends to be Rosalind so that he/she can seduce, frustrate and entertain Orlando.

4 The value of silence: With Rosalind talking so brilliantly and Orlando supplying many of her cues, it is easy to forget that Celia too is on stage. We can watch the scene through her on-stage role as audience. She reminds 'Ganymede' of the Rosalind that lies beneath and can remain a conventional woman as foil to Rosalind's subversive experiments. Does she partially share in the games, resent Rosalind's happy exuberance, or feel alarmed that playfulness is being pushed towards dangerous extremes? She speaks very briefly in this extract. At first she 'cannot say the words': is this refusal or inadequacy?

From *Measure for Measure*

The Duke has dropped his Friar's disguise and is now giving his judgements on the mixture before him of criminals and virtuous citizens. He has forced Angelo to marry Mariana but has still condemned him to death. He has sacked the Provost for having apparently beheaded Claudio and requires the reprobate Barnardine to be brought before him. It appears that he is taking a hard moral and judicial line on everyone who has fallen short. These are the final lines of the play.

ESCALUS	I am sorry one so learned and so wise
	As you, Lord Angelo, have still appeared,
	Should slip so grossly, both in the heat of blood
	And lack of tempered judgement afterward.
ANGELO	I am sorry that such sorrow I procure, 5
	And so deep sticks it in my penitent heart
	That I crave death more willingly than mercy.
	'Tis my deserving, and I do entreat it.

Enter BARNARDINE, PROVOST, CLAUDIO [*muffled*] *and* JULIET

DUKE	Which is that Barnardine?
PROVOST	This, my lord.
DUKE	There was a friar told me of this man. 10
	Sirrah, thou art said to have a stubborn soul
	That apprehends no further than this world,
	And squar'st thy life according. Thou'rt condemned:
	But, for those earthly faults, I quit them all,
	And pray thee take this mercy to provide 15
	For better times to come. Friar, advise him,
	I leave him to your hand. – What muffled fellow's that?

PROVOST This is another prisoner that I saved,
          Who should have died when Claudio lost his head,
          As like almost to Claudio as himself.   20

                    [*He unmuffles Claudio*]

DUKE   [*To Isabella*] If he be like your brother, for his sake
          Is he pardoned, and for your lovely sake
          Give me your hand, and say you will be mine,
          He is my brother too. But fitter time for that.
          By this Lord Angelo perceives he's safe;   25
          Methinks I see a quick'ning in his eye.
          Well, Angelo, your evil quits you well.
          Look that you love your wife: her worth, worth yours.
          I find an apt remission in myself;
          And yet here's one in place I cannot pardon,   30
          [*To Lucio*] You, sirrah, that knew me for a fool, a coward,
          One all of luxury, an ass, a madman:
          Wherein have I so deserved of you
          That you extol me thus?

LUCIO   'Faith, my lord, I spoke it but according to the trick: if you   35
          will hang me for it, you may – but I had rather it would please
          you I might be whipped.

DUKE   Whipped first, sir, and hanged after.
          Proclaim it, provost, round about the city:
          If any woman wronged by this lewd fellow,   40
          As I have heard him swear himself there's one
          Whom he begot with child, let her appear,
          And he shall marry her. The nuptial finished,
          Let him be whipped and hanged.

LUCIO   I beseech your highness, do not marry me to a whore. Your   45
          highness said, even now, I made you a duke: good my
          lord, do not recompense me in making me a cuckold.

DUKE   Upon mine honour, thou shalt marry her.
          Thy slanders I forgive, and therewithal
          Remit thy other forfeits: take him to prison,   50
          And see our pleasure herein executed.

LUCIO   Marrying a punk, my lord, is pressing to death, whipping, and
          hanging!

DUKE   Slandering a prince deserves it.
          She, Claudio, that you wronged, look you restore.   55
          Joy to you, Mariana! Love her, Angelo!
          I have confessed her, and I know her virtue.
          Thanks, good friend Escalus, for thy much goodness;
          There's more behind, that is more gratulate.

Thanks, provost, for thy care and secrecy,   60
We shall employ thee in a worthier place.
Forgive him, Angelo, that brought you home
The head of Ragozine for Claudio's;
Th'offence pardons itself. Dear Isabel,
I have a motion much imports your good,   65
Whereto, if you'll a willing ear incline,
What's mine is yours, and what is yours is mine.
So bring us to our palace, where we'll show
What's yet behind that's meet you all should know.

                                        [*Exeunt*]
                              (Act 5 Scene 1: lines 463–531)

Performance issues

1   How does an audience now regard Angelo? He dominated Acts 1 and 2, he has
    been proved a murderous hypocrite, but Mariana has accepted him with all his
    faults. He says nothing for the play's last 60 lines. His silence is puzzling, but
    may be eloquent in performance. His final words request death but does he still
    feel this way at the end of the play?

2   It may seem odd that so much of this final section deals with the problem
    of Lucio. (You might make a similar comment about Malvolio at the end of
    Twelfth Night.) He also answers back more than the other characters in their
    predicaments. Why does the Duke punish him so severely, then appear to
    change his mind? Does Lucio present a problem in Vienna that is different from
    anyone else?

3   By 1604 (the date of this play) audiences might well expect the last lines of
    Shakespeare's comedies to be complicated in tone and atmosphere. Offers
    of marriage give cause for optimism, but what happens when the girl, here
    Isabella, remains silent? Does she accept the offer, reject it, or remain non-
    committal? How does she react to the others on stage? How does the Duke
    react to her silence? Bear in mind that this is a very public scene – or may some
    of it be private? There are many different decisions to be made about silent
    behaviour in these last lines.

4   There are further silences. Barnardine says nothing when the Duke describes
    his life, nor when he is offered mercy. Claudio says nothing to Isabella when
    he is unmuffled (line 31), nor she to him – remember the circumstances of
    their last meeting. Does Juliet play any part in the reunions? Some productions
    follow the earlier references to her pregnancy by having her now cradling a
    child.

5   Amongst these silences the Duke does most of the talking. Is this a sign of
    authority or neurotic weakness? How optimistic is this ending?

From *Macbeth*

Macbeth has gained the crown by murdering his guest, King Duncan. He then
realises that his fellow general, Banquo, is quietly suspicious of the crime. He has
urged Banquo not to miss the banquet he is providing for his chief noblemen, but
then secretly arranges for Banquo and his son to be murdered. The banquet takes
place and Macbeth pretends to be concerned about Banquo's absence, at which
Banquo's ghost, streaked with blood, appears with silent accusation. No-one else
can see the ghost, but Macbeth's strange and violent behaviour alarms everyone.
Lady Macbeth soothes her husband and he prepares again to play the generous
host.

	Come, love and health to all,	
	Then I'll sit down. Give me some wine; fill full!	
	Enter Ghost [of Banquo]	
	I drink to th'general joy o'th'whole table,	
	And to our dear friend Banquo, whom we miss.	
	Would he were here! To all, and him we thirst,	5
	And all to all.	
LORDS	Our duties and the pledge.	
MACBETH	Avaunt and quit my sight! Let the earth hide thee!	
	Thy bones are marrowless, thy blood is cold;	
	Thou hast no speculation in those eyes	
	Which thou dost glare with.	
LADY MACBETH	Think of this, good peers,	10
	But as a thing of custom. 'Tis no other,	
	Only it spoils the pleasure of the time.	
MACBETH	What man dare, I dare;	
	Approach thou like the rugged Russian bear,	
	The armed rhinoceros, or th'Hyrcan tiger,	15
	Take any shape but that, and my firm nerves	
	Shall never tremble. Or be alive again,	
	And dare me to the desert with thy sword;	
	If trembling I inhabit then, protest me	
	The baby of a girl. Hence horrible shadow,	20
	Unreal mock'ry hence.	
	[Exit Ghost of Banquo]	
	Why so, being gone,	
	I am a man again. – Pray you, sit still.	

LADY MACBETH You have displaced the mirth, broke the good
                meeting
          With most admired disorder.
MACBETH   Can such things be,
          And overcome us like a summer's cloud,   25
          Without our special wonder? You make me strange
          Even to the disposition that I owe,
          When now I think you can behold such sights
          And keep the natural ruby of your cheeks,
          When mine is blanched with fear.
ROSS   What sights, my lord?   30
LADY MACBETH I pray you speak not; he grows worse and worse.
          Question enrages him. At once, good night.
          Stand not upon the order of your going,
          But go at once.
LENNOX   Good night, and better health
          Attend his majesty.
LADY MACBETH   A kind good night to all.   35

                            [*Exeunt*] *Lords* [*and Attendants*]

MACBETH   It will have blood they say: blood will have blood.
          Stones have been known to move and trees to speak.
          Augures, and understood relations, have
          By maggot-pies, and choughs, and rooks brought forth
          The secret'st man of blood. What is the night?   40
LADY MACBETH Almost at odds with morning, which is which.
MACBETH   How sayst thou that Macduff denies his person
          At our great bidding?
LADY MACBETH   Did you send to him, sir?
MACBETH   I hear it by the way, but I will send.
          There's not a one of them but in his house   45
          I keep a servant feed. I will tomorrow –
          And betimes I will – to the weïrd sisters.
          More shall they speak. For now I am bent to know
          By the worst means, the worst; for mine own good,
          All causes shall give way. I am in blood   50
          Stepped in so far that should I wade no more,
          Returning were as tedious as go o'er.
          Strange things I have in head that will to hand,
          Which must be acted ere they may be scanned.
LADY MACBETH You lack the season of all natures, sleep.   55

MACBETH	Come, we'll to sleep. My strange and self-abuse
	Is the initiate fear that wants hard use;
	We are yet but young in deed.

Exeunt

(Act 3 Scene 4: lines 87–144)

Performance issues

1 Scale of the occasion? The banquet (or 'feast') is the first public ceremony of Macbeth's reign when he can display lavish entertainment. Some directors stress the grandeur of intention so that his embarrassing behaviour will be more striking. Others see the whole play as suffocatingly claustrophobic and design this scene to match his trapped mind.

2 The Ghost's appearance is a moment of shock and theatrical ingenuity. Banquo's Ghost has already appeared (line 48), then disappeared. Macbeth's alarm and rage then lasts for 35 lines. The audience will expect a second appearance as soon as Macbeth refers to 'our dear friend, Banquo', but this time the reaction is only 15 lines. How does Shakespeare make the language of this second appearance different? How can directors and actors ensure that this second haunting is equally gripping and not just a repeat of the first? In his 1890 production William Poel brought on the ghost of Duncan, not Banquo, at this point.

3 The Lords depart. Lady Macbeth refers to 'the order of your going', which may indicate that some formal procedure is beginning, which would make a deeper mockery of a situation that has already descended into shambles. Directors and actors need to consider (a) to what extent Lady Macbeth has taken charge of a situation that may have left her husband exhausted and incapable of decision, (b) how the departure is staged and (c) if any noblemen have inferred that Macbeth is a criminal as well as being deeply disturbed.

4 Communication between husband and wife: Many modern productions isolate the two from each other, even from the start of Act 3. She reaches out to him, but he seems incapable of response. Actors and director working on this play need to trace sensitively the course of the relationship. The final moments of this scene are crucial. Are they communicating? Or is Macbeth engaged in a monologue which she fails to penetrate? In some productions husband and wife leave together clinging to each other; in some she is left alone, either evidently broken or grimly resuming her throne like an impassive icon.

From *Cymbeline*

Against her father's wishes, the princess Imogen has married Posthumus. He has
taken flight to Rome where, with a group of young men, he praises Imogen's beauty
and honour. One of them, Iachimo, sets himself the challenge to go to England
and to seduce her. Imogen greets him graciously as a friend of Posthumus and
agrees to keep safe in her bedroom a trunk (supposedly containing their presents
for the emperor). Meanwhile, the arrogant Cloten, son to the Queen (Imogen's
stepmother), is trying unsuccessfully to win her love. This extract starts at the
beginning of Act 2 Scene 2.

IMOGEN	Who's there? My woman Helen?	
LADY	Please you, madam.	
IMOGEN	What hour is it?	
LADY	Almost midnight, madam.	
IMOGEN	I have read three hours then. Mine eyes are weak;	
	Fold down the leaf where I have left. To bed.	
	Take not away the taper, leave it burning;	5
	And if thou canst awake by four o'th'clock,	
	I prithee call me. Sleep hath seized me wholly.	

[*Exit Lady*]

	To your protection I commend me, gods.	
	From fairies and the tempters of the night	
	Guard me, beseech ye. *Sleeps*	10

IACHIMO [*comes*] *from the trunk*

IACHIMO	The crickets sing, and man's o'er-laboured sense	
	Repairs itself by rest. Our Tarquin thus	
	Did softly press the rushes, ere he wakened	
	The chastity he wounded. Cytherea,	
	How bravely thou becom'st thy bed! Fresh lily,	15
	And whiter than the sheets! That I might touch,	
	But kiss, one kiss! Rubies unparagoned,	
	How dearly they do't! 'Tis her breathing that	
	Perfumes the chamber thus. The flame o'th'taper	
	Bows toward her, and would underpeep her lids	20
	To see th'enclosèd lights, now canopied	
	Under these windows, white and azure laced	
	With blue of heaven's own tinct. But my design –	
	To note the chamber. I will write all down.	

[*Takes out his notebook*]

	Such and such pictures; there the window; such	25

Th'adornment of her bed; the arras, figures,
Why, such and such; and the contents o'th'story.
Ah, but some natural notes about her body
Above ten thousand meaner movables
Would testify, t'enrich mine inventory.   30
O sleep, thou ape of death, lie dull upon her,
And be her sense but as a monument,
Thus in a chapel lying. Come off, come off –

          [Taking off her bracelet]

As slippery as the Gordian knot was hard!
'Tis mine, and this will witness outwardly,   35
As strongly as the conscience does within,
To th'madding of her lord. On her left breast
A mole cinque-spotted, like the crimson drops
I'th'bottom of a cowslip. Here's a voucher,
Stronger than ever law could make; this secret   40
Will force him think I have picked the lock and ta'en
The treasure of her honour. No more. To what end?
Why should I write this down that's riveted,
Screwed to my memory? She hath been reading late
The tale of Tereus; here the leaf's turned down   45
Where Philomel gave up. I have enough;
To th'trunk again, and shut the spring of it.
Swift, swift, you dragons of the night, that dawning
May bare the raven's eye! I lodge in fear;
Though this a heavenly angel, hell is here.   50

                    Clock strikes

One, two, three: time, time!   *Exit [into the trunk]*

[The trunk is carried off, and the bed withdrawn]

2.3 *Enter* CLOTEN *and [the two]* LORDS

FIRST LORD Your lordship is the most patient man in loss, the most
            coldest that ever turned up ace.
CLOTEN   It would make any man cold to lose.
FIRST LORD But not every man patient after the noble temper of your
            lordship. You are most hot and furious when you win.   5
CLOTEN   Winning will put any man into courage. If I could get this
            foolish Imogen, I should have gold enough. It's almost
            morning, is't not?
FIRST LORD Day, my lord.
CLOTEN   I would this music would come. I am advised to give her   10
            music o'mornings; they say it will penetrate.

Enter MUSICIANS

Come on, tune. If you can penetrate her with your
fingering, so; we'll try with tongue too. If none will do, let
her remain; but I'll never give o'er. First, a very excellent
good-conceited thing; after, a wonderful sweet air, with   15
admirable rich words to it; and then let her consider.

[*Music*]

MUSICIAN   (*Sings*) Hark, hark, the lark at heaven's gate sings,
      And Phoebus 'gins arise,
  His steeds to water at those springs
      On chaliced flowers that lies,   20
  And winking Mary-buds begin to ope their golden eyes;
  With everything that pretty is, my lady sweet, arise;
        Arise, arise!

(Act 2 Scene 2: lines 1–51; Scene 3: lines 1–23)

Performance issues

1   Time and light: These two scenes run from midnight to dawn and contain
the play's crucial event that causes the misunderstanding between Imogen
and Posthumus. There are several references to darkness, time passing, the
flickering taper, all of which may have symbolic as well as literal value. You can
imagine how a film might convey atmosphere and significance. In the theatre
there is a range of possibilities from the daylit Globe to an enclosed modern
studio. Consider how different theatre spaces might influence a director's
choices.

2   The details firstly of the bedchamber and then of Imogen's body are extremely
precise. This is because Iachimo is determined to sound convincingly intimate
when he returns to Rome with his lie of seducing Imogen. Does an audience
have to see the details too? How far does a set design need to go towards full
realism?

3   Props: Several are mentioned: bed, book, taper, trunk, notebook, bracelet.
Consider their relative importance to both plot and theme – and the decisions
a designer might make about how to show them.

4   Music: This extract ends with a beautiful aubade (a dawn song), but
Shakespeare associates it with the unpleasant Cloten who has brought the
musicians to Imogen's door. In some productions Cloten even sings this
song himself. (In *The Tempest* there is a similar surprise when brutish
Caliban has the finest ear for music.) Consider the value of this music in the

relationship of these two contrasting scenes. Note that the song emerges from some of Cloten's crude punning: 'penetrate', 'fingering', 'tongue' (Scene 3, lines 12–13).

From *The Tempest*

Caliban has led the drunk Stephano and Trinculo through the swamps and briars to Prospero's cell so that they can murder him. Stephano and Trinculo are distracted by a display of fine clothes, but Caliban is anxious about the delay. The extract starts towards the end of Act 4.

TRINCULO	Monster, come put some lime upon your fingers, and away with the rest.	
CALIBAN	I will have none on't. We shall lose our time,	
	And all be turned to barnacles, or to apes	
	With foreheads villainous low.	5
STEPHANO	Monster, lay to your fingers. Help to bear this away where	
	my hogshead of wine is, or I'll turn you out of my kingdom.	
	[*Loading Caliban with garments*] Go to, carry this.	
TRINCULO	And this.	
STEPHANO	Ay, and this.	10

A noise of hunters heard. Enter diverse spirits in shape of dogs and hounds, hunting them about, Prospero and Ariel setting them on

PROSPERO	Hey, Mountain, hey!	
ARIEL	Silver! There it goes, Silver.	
PROSPERO	Fury, Fury! There, Tyrant, there! Hark, hark!	

[*Exeunt Caliban, Stephano and Trinculo, pursued by spirits*]

	[*To Ariel*] Go, charge my goblins that they grind their joints	
	With dry convulsions, shorten up their sinews	
	With agèd cramps, and more pinch-spotted make them,	15
	Than pard, or cat-o'-mountain.	
ARIEL	Hark, they roar.	
PROSPERO	Let them be hunted soundly. At this hour	
	Lies at my mercy all mine enemies.	
	Shortly shall all my labours end, and thou	
	Shalt have the air at freedom. For a little	20
	Follow, and do me service.	

Exeunt

Act 5 Scene 1
Near Prospero's cave

Enter PROSPERO, *in his magic robes, and* ARIEL

PROSPERO Now does my project gather to a head.
My charms crack not, my spirits obey, and Time
Goes upright with his carriage. How's the day?

ARIEL On the sixth hour; at which time, my lord,
You said our work should cease.

PROSPERO   I did say so,   5
When first I raised the tempest. Say, my spirit,
How fares the king and's followers?

ARIEL   Confined together
In the same fashion as you gave in charge,
Just as you left them; all prisoners, sir,
In the line-grove which weather-fends your cell;   10
They cannot budge till your release. The king,
His brother, and yours, abide all three distracted,
And the remainder mourning over them,
Brim full of sorrow and dismay; but chiefly
Him that you termed, sir, the good old lord Gonzalo.   15
His tears runs down his beard like winter's drops
From eaves of reeds. Your charm so strongly works 'em
That if you now beheld them, your affections
Would become tender.

PROSPERO   Dost thou think so, spirit?

ARIEL Mine would, sir, were I human.

PROSPERO   And mine shall.   20
Hast thou, which art but air, a touch, a feeling
Of their afflictions, and shall not myself,
One of their kind, that relish all as sharply
Passion as they, be kindlier moved than thou art?
Though with their high wrongs I am struck to th'quick, 25
Yet, with my nobler reason, 'gainst my fury
Do I take part. The rarer action is
In virtue, than in vengeance. They being penitent,
The sole drift of my purpose doth extend
Not a frown further. Go, release them, Ariel.   30
My charms I'll break, their senses I'll restore,
And they shall be themselves.

ARIEL   I'll fetch them, sir.   *Exit*
(Act 4 Scene 1: lines 240–260; Act 5 Scene 1: lines 1–32)

Performance issues

1   Stage directions: As director what detailed directions would you write in your own production notes that cope with (a) the chase and (b) the scene change, bearing in mind that Prospero and Ariel end Act 4 and begin Act 5? Would you have them leave the stage?

2   The chase clearly terrifies Stephano, Trinculo and Caliban, who are hunted like wild animals. Should it amuse or alarm an audience?

3   Prospero and Ariel: Their relationship is an important strand in how you interpret the play as a whole. In some productions Prospero holds constant authority (as suggested here in his 'magic robes'). But Ariel has special powers and here he goes beyond the role of obedient servant when he presumes to teach Prospero about human affections (line 11 in Act 5 Scene 1). In some productions Prospero can sense Ariel's presence but can't see him. How would you stage their dialogue to express the possibly complicated matter of who is dominant?

5 | How to write about Shakespeare on stage

- Should performance explain or simply explore the meaning of a scene or passage?

- How can discussion of performance on stage support a literary analysis of the play on the page?

- Can reviews of individual productions offer general insights into the plays?

- What are the criteria for reviewing a review?

Here are three ways in which you may be asked to write about Shakespeare on stage:

1   To explore the meaning and impact of a passage or scene from a play.

2   To support a literary essay on aspects of a Shakespeare play.

3   A review of a performance you have seen (and reviewing other reviews).

Writing about a passage or scene from a play

Whatever the focus of your writing, you should always remember that Shakespeare wrote plays for an audience to see and hear on stage. So attention to his stagecraft will improve your own understanding and writing. This means considering the plays' theatrical qualities: the effects produced by means other than ideas, characters and imagery. What stage directions may be implied from the writing? Aspects of stagecraft include opportunities for spectacle, timing, tension, contrast, the presentation of conflict and passion, climax, anticlimax, dramatic irony. You can support your views by referring to theatre history: how effects were achieved in Shakespeare's theatre (see Part 1), and in theatres that have staged his plays since then (see Parts 2 and 3).

Each extract or scene conveys meaning from its context as well as within itself. What came immediately before it? What events, thoughts and feelings do the characters bring to the drama of this particular moment? Are they all being open and honest with each other? What does the silence of some characters contribute? You should be aware of the variety within Shakespeare's stagecraft: his mixing of public and private scenes, the context of soliloquies, changes of tempo between measured moments and rapid, tense scenes.

▶ Choose the play you know best. Reread the final 100 lines or so. Use the two paragraphs above to help you to identify the elements of stagecraft which ensure the scene has a significant effect on the audience.

▶ Collaboration with others is essential when working towards a performance: it is also often very helpful when you become the critic of a performance. If another student is working on the same play as you, each may choose an extract of 40–70 lines and ask the sort of questions suggested in Part 4, Extracts and performance issues. Hand the list of questions to your partner. Using these questions, you each write an analysis of how a director might approach the extract for performance.

The 20th-century poet and playwright T.S. Eliot aimed to revive verse drama, to use the language of poetry in a functional way and not as a decorative embellishment. In his 1950 lecture *Poetry and Drama* he argued that the verse 'will only be "poetry" when the dramatic situation has reached such a point of intensity that poetry becomes the natural utterance'. He wanted the verse rhythm to have its effect on the hearers without their being conscious that a special type of language was being used. He then examined the first scene of *Hamlet*. He pointed to the variety of style (brusque, eerie, sonorous, staccato, reflective) and believed it has the special merit that 'there is no line of poetry which is not justified by its dramatic value'.

▶ Reread the opening scene of a play you know well. Bear in mind that the audience may come with no knowledge of the story or characters. Examine how Shakespeare's language and the techniques of his stagecraft engage the audience's attention and lead them into the story.

Using performance as part of a literary essay on Shakespeare

As a student you will be encouraged to pay attention to the relevant contexts for whatever literary texts you are reading. These will include social, historical and cultural aspects of the period in which it was written. For example, when reading *Macbeth*, you will enrich your response to the play if you learn more about the following: concepts of tragedy; Elizabethan and Jacobean attitudes to the monarchy; witchcraft; the status of women; Holinshed's *Chronicles*, which provided most of Shakespeare's source material.

Performance is also a relevant context. It may be argued that it is the most important because the script never reaches its fullest life until the play appears on stage. Part 1 gives you some insights into the contexts of theatre conditions and stagecraft which influenced Shakespeare's writing of the plays around 1600. Later sections tell you about important aspects of his theatre afterlife, because Shakespeare is continually reinvented and received in different ways. You may also wish to consider opera, musicals, dance, film and TV, all of which lie outside the scope of this book, but they are still performances, all expressing Shakespeare, and often reaching wider audiences than the live theatre can.

Performance as context: *The Tempest*

Suppose, for example, you are studying *The Tempest* and you have been asked to focus on the contrast between base and noble behaviour. It will be helpful to examine the contrast in Act 1, when Miranda is disgusted by Caliban, then delighted by her first sight of Ferdinand, the prince.

What sort of impressions, physical and moral, should Caliban make in this first appearance? Prospero's treatment of him is frustrated, angry and abusive – and to some extent, your thinking about Prospero conditions your view of Caliban. Can Prospero – a duke, a philosopher, deeply versed in natural magic, and (in many productions) possessing almost superhuman wisdom – be misguided about Caliban? Or are Miranda and Prospero unfairly prejudiced? In post-colonial times, should an audience regard Caliban as a 'noble savage', exploited, abused and deprived of his rightful inheritance?

As Caliban leaves, the mysterious music of Ariel's song leads Ferdinand on stage. Both characters are, in different ways, suitors to Miranda. Peter Hall, in his 1975 production at The Old Vic, left Caliban far upstage gazing out to sea. When (apparently) the same character, dressed in animal skins, turned round, the audience was amazed to see that it was Ferdinand, not Caliban, who then moved downstage. This lavish production, which evoked Jacobean masque, was making a Renaissance point about man in his capacity to range from sophisticated prince to base animal. How might other interpretations of these two characters lead you to different visual versions of this moment?

In this scene, Ferdinand is led, attended and closely watched. Most royal figures are 'on stage' for much of their lives. Prospero urges Miranda 'The fringed curtains of thine eye advance …'. Does she see a supremely noble prince, or a passive victim? Does she see a desperate young man lashing out at his emotional and physical predicament? Does Prospero welcome him as an ideal suitor for Miranda, or is he potentially another Caliban? Music constantly provides atmosphere in *The Tempest* and here gives emotional colour to Ferdinand's arrival. You need to decide whether it disturbs, reassures or creates mystery, or a subtle mixture of all three.

Reading the play in this way to recall or imagine it on stage is also a type of critical analysis (see Part 4, Extracts and performance issues). The director and actors constantly give their version of what Shakespeare's play means; then they use their performance skills to convince you, just as literary critics use their writing to persuade you into accepting their interpretation of a book or poem.

Performance should offer you four benefits:

- a context for understanding the play

- a criticism to help you interpret it

- a completion of what existed merely as a script

- two to three hours of stimulating enjoyment (and this is the real point of performance).

Reviewing a performance – and reviewing the reviews

The first thing to be said is that there is no single or 'right' way to present Shakespeare on stage. Evidence from the earlier sections of this book should indicate that very different approaches to a particular play can all be successful in entertaining and gripping audiences. You may also feel that some approaches may now be very dated; others may be too eagerly searching for popularity in cheap and narrow ways. You may, for example, support Hamlet's distaste for crude over-playing and too much licence for clowning. The audience may laugh, though as Hamlet himself says, 'in the meantime some necessary question of the play be then to be considered'. You will probably feel, with Hamlet, that the play and the (long dead) playwright sometimes need protection.

In the first instance, try to distinguish between the quality of performance and the intentions behind the interpretations. If actors can't be heard, if they move clumsily, if the lighting is over-fussy or leaves actors in the dark, all these are signs of poor technique and deserve to be criticised. However, you may find some newspaper reviews hostile or dismissive without being clear about precisely what they condemn. A few reviewers enjoy being severe or sneeringly witty, as though they and their reputation are more important than the play. But most try to be fair: actors are vulnerable, they are engaged in a difficult task and deserve an audience predisposed in their favour. An audience should always go to the theatre in a responsive frame of mind, expecting that the play will engage its mind and emotions.

If you know the play well, you will probably look closely for details you expect to see, and admire a production that fits your preconceptions. The danger may come when the director and actors treat the play in ways that surprise you. Are you being fair to their unfamiliar insights? Are you prepared to treat them as you would a teacher or critic who has suggested a new idea about the play? This doesn't mean that fine acting is all that is required. You must still use your judgement and decide on the qualities of this new interpretation. Is it illuminating, or is it misguided, trendy, gimmicky or limiting? To make these judgements you need to know the play's text and refer to it in your review.

Now for the practical aspects of your writing. You can't refer to everything. Like the professional reviewer, you probably have a word limit. You must record your strongest impressions and these should be connected to the most important aspects of the play. But don't dwell in generalities. Be true to your feelings in the theatre when you responded to precise moments: perhaps two characters in contact, a soliloquy, a dramatic silence, an aspect of design that illuminated something in the play.

Reviewing the reviews: *Macbeth*

In 2007 the small studio theatre at Chichester staged *Macbeth*. Here are two newspaper reviews, of similar length, from the *Guardian:*

(a) One of the most exciting current partnerships between actor and director can now be caught at Chichester. Rupert Goold, the young artistic director of Headlong Theatre, has directed Patrick Stewart, at the peak of his considerable powers as a Shakespearean actor, before, in an unforgettable arctic *Tempest*. The *Macbeth* they have created is even more explosive.

It's worth going just for the opening scene. A soldier gasps for breath on a hospital trolley; he's surrounded by walls of white, lavatory-style tiles and tended by silent, masked nurses. He gives news of the battle and Macbeth's bravery and fades away. As he does so, those ministering angels wheel round, to reveal themselves as heralds of death: these carers are witches, who will forever hover ambiguously around the action. 'To win us to our harm, the instruments of darkness tell us truths'; this is the scariest of Shakespeare plays, in which woods have feet and ghosts are guests.

Goold's production doesn't stint on gore. Dead fowl are heaped up for a banquet; a tap runs red; great gouts of blood spread across the walls. The action takes place in what could be a butcher's shop, or a modernist kitchen, with a heavy industrial lift which slams down to allow frightful entrances, and weirdly whisks apparitions away to lower depths.

It doesn't stint on significance, either: a video screen flashes footage of military parades from the former Soviet Union. The carnage in the castle looks like the symptom of a nationwide disturbance. It also looks like the outward sign of psychological disorder. As Lady Macbeth, Kate Fleetwood is magnetic, sexually predatory, quick to action and as quickly dashed. Stewart, a martial presence and a mellifluous speaker, finds a strange croak in his voice as the action darkens; when he talks of the rooky wood, it's as if a raven is beating in his throat. Michael Feast's distinguished Macduff, hearing of his family's slaughter, lets fall a desolating long silence. Episode upon episode is fruitfully re-thought: the scene in which the dead Banquo appears to Macbeth is played twice, once as seen through his host's eyes, once through the eyes of the feasting guests. Every moment throws up something terrifying.

(Susannah Clapp in the *Guardian*, 10 June 2007)

(b) Rupert Goold is the intemperately exciting young director who gave us a sensational *Tempest* last year at Stratford. Now, reunited with Patrick Stewart, he has come up with an equally astonishing *Macbeth*: one that is fiercely conceptual, in its evocations of both Soviet tyranny and gothic horror, but spoken with crystalline clarity and keeps the spectators on the edges of their seats.

Anthony Ward's white-walled, underground setting suggests a mixture of abattoir, kitchen and military hospital. Its prime feature is an iron-gated lift in which characters either descend to, or flee from, the Macbeths' subterranean hell. As Macbeth achieves power through a military coup, we see projections of massed troops marching through what looks like Red Square. Meanwhile, Banquo's murder is accomplished by sinister figures on a night train to nowhere, evoked by a few chairs and Adam Cork's eerie sound-design.

Other directors, such as Max Stafford-Clark and Greg Doran, have highlighted the militaristic nature of Macbeth's regime. Goold pushes it further by suggesting that Macbeth emerges from a dictatorship in which Duncan is accompanied by goose-stepping troops.

Patrick Stewart, without minimising Macbeth's evil, excellently highlights the paranoia that accompanies power. He eyes Banquo nervously from the start. Even when dressing for dinner with his wife, he seems haunted by fear. And Stewart never lets us forget that Macbeth, uniquely among Shakespeare's villains, is morbidly aware of what he has sacrificed: like Olivier, Stewart allows his voice to soar when describing the 'troops of friends' he knows he will never enjoy.

The potential danger of Goold's approach is that it reinforces Malcolm's description of the Macbeths as 'this dead butcher and his fiend-like queen'. But Goold shows that tyranny, however insecure, is still based on slaughter. The idea is brilliantly underlined when Kate Fleetwood's terrifying Lady Macbeth seeks to cleanse her hands under a kitchen tap that runs blood-red water.

Goold takes other justifiable liberties, so that Michael Feast's Macduff turns up at the Macbeths' house-party with his family only to bundle them away after the murder. And the England scene is wittily staged, with Scott Handy's Malcolm discovered attending a musical soiree that contrasts strongly with the Macbeths' own brutal banquet barn-dance. But that is typical of a production which, by its imaginative inventiveness, makes you experience the play anew.

(Michael Billington in the *Guardian*, 4 June 2007)

You will probably find interesting similarities and differences between these two reviews. Here are some suggestions to help you to consider them.

▶ The production impressed both reviewers. But praise (and fault finding too) doesn't in itself guarantee an effective review, though the theatre's marketing manager hopes to read praise. In these reviews, do you find the praise precise and does it lead you to consider the core of the play?

▶ Both reviewers use vivid language to describe physical effects. Is this appropriate for *Macbeth* – and would it be equally so for other Shakespeare plays?

▶ Consider the amount of space the reviewers give to:
- the play's ideas and themes
- how the director deals with scenes and incidents
- the visual effects, and the language
- the different characters and the quality of the acting.

Reviewing the reviews: *King Lear*
You may feel that different types of play need different approaches. Here is an extract from Michael Billington's review of *King Lear* (Royal Shakespeare Company, July 1990):

Confronted by this vast, unwieldy play, Mr Hytner is too wily to offer a confining concept. I do, however, see a consistent idea running through his production: an exploration of the insane contradictions of a world where the gods are seen as both just and wantonly cruel, where nature is both purifying and destructive. The fashionable view is that King Lear is an essay in Beckettesque nihilism. Mr Hytner, to his credit, treats it as a tragi-comedy full of turbulent paradox.

You see this in David Fielding's excellent set ... a revolving, open-sided cube that during the storm scene gives on to a dizzying skyscape. Order opens up to reveal chaos. And the same pattern is visible in erratic human behaviour. Lear, having cursed Goneril with sterility, rushes back to embrace her. Astonishingly, Regan first conspires in the blinding of Gloucester and then tenderly asks him, rather than her wounded husband, 'How dost, my lord?' Mr Hytner ushers us into a morally topsy-turvy universe in which good and evil frequently cohabit within the same person.

I take this to be the clue to John Wood's ground-breaking Lear. He does not offer a simple linear reading in which folly leads to madness and thence to moral regeneration: Wood's Lear exists in a permanent state of spiritual schizophrenia. You see this in the brilliantly played first scene where he enters clutching the trisected map like a berserk geography master and then drifts into aphasia. Equally powerful is the way his rage against Cordelia is short-circuited by his love: 'Better thou hadst not been born,' he ferociously cries and then chokes, unable to finish the sentence.

As you would expect from Mr Wood, it is a highly original reading that notches up point after point. In the hovel scenes, he has a crazed sprightliness pursuing Poor Tom ('Thou art the thing itself') with the ecstasy of a scientist making a Eureka-like discovery, But perhaps his best moment comes when he promises the imprisoned Cordelia that they will take upon them 'the mystery of things'.

It is a performance that destroys the barrier between madness and sanity: this Lear occupies both territories at once. What for me excludes it, as yet, from the select club of great Lears is that it wants the gift of pathos. It is an intriguing, daring, pioneering performance, but also one that is somewhat over-calculated. Mr Wood at the moment is superbly playing Lear. What he has to learn to do is to let Lear play him.

(Michael Billington, in the *Guardian*, July 1990)

▶ Is this a helpful review? What are its strengths in communicating the life of the production (for example, set, direction, stage business, acting)? Does this reviewer point to any new or postmodern interpretations of the play? (See Part 3, page 81.) Does the review make you rethink your own ideas about the play?

▶ Collect several newspaper reviews of a recent production (and, if you have seen the play before reading these reviews, write your own and add it to the collection). Which review contains the most insights? And which is the most sweeping and shallow? Give reasons for your decisions.

▶ Do you think critics make an important contribution to theatre? Or are they merely 'parasites clinging on to the creativity of others'?

6 | Resources

Chronology

1564	Birth of William Shakespeare
1572	Act for Restraining Vagabonds
1576	The Theatre built in Shoreditch
1592	Shakespeare *King Richard III*
1594	Shakespeare *Romeo and Juliet*
1595	Shakespeare *A Midsummer Night's Dream*
1596	Shakespeare *The Merchant of Venice*
1599	The Globe built in Southwark
	Shakespeare *As You Like It*, *Henry V*, *Julius Caesar*
1601	Shakespeare *Hamlet*
1603	Elizabeth I dies; James VI of Scotland becomes James I of England
1604	Shakespeare *Measure for Measure*, *Othello*
1605	Shakespeare *King Lear*
1606	Shakespeare *Macbeth*
1610	Shakespeare *The Tempest*
1616	Death of Shakespeare
1623	First Folio edition of Shakespeare's plays
1642	Theatres closed
1649	Execution of Charles I; Oliver Cromwell installed as Lord Protector of the Commonwealth
1660	The Restoration of the Monarchy: Charles II
1683	Nahum Tate's version of *King Lear*
1725	Alexander Pope's edition of *Shakespeare's Plays*

1747–1766	David Garrick's company at Drury Lane Theatre
1769	David Garrick's Shakespeare Jubilee in Stratford
1818	Thomas Bowdler *A Family Shakespeare in Ten Volumes*
1878–1902	Henry Irving's company at The Lyceum Theatre
1879	The Shakespeare Memorial Theatre opens in Stratford
1894	Foundation of the Elizabethan Stage Society
1904	Publication of Philip Henslowe's papers and diaries
1960	Shakespeare Memorial Theatre renamed as The Royal Shakespeare Theatre
1986	The Swan Theatre opens in Stratford
1995	First season of the Shakespeare's Globe Theatre at Southwark

Further reading

Harley Granville Barker *Prefaces to Shakespeare* (Heinemann Drama, 1995)
A great director's analysis of Shakespeare's plays for their structure and stagecraft.

Jonathan Bate *The Genius of Shakespeare* (Picador, 1997)
A stimulating biography of Shakespeare's talent and reputation, plus lively discussion of the way his plays have influenced other writers, artists, composers.

Jonathan Bate and Eric Rasmussen, eds. *The RSC Shakespeare: The Complete Works* (Macmillan, 2007)
Essential as a version for today of Shakespeare's First Folio of 1623, including a very informative and accessible introduction surveying the theatre practice of Shakespeare's times and a brief essay on each of the plays.

A.C. Bradley *Shakespearean Tragedy* (Penguin, 1991)
First published in 1904. The most important source of 'character criticism'.

J.S. Bratton & Julie Hankey, series eds. *Shakespeare in Production* (Cambridge University Press)
This series gives detailed stage histories of individual Shakespeare texts.

A.R. Braunmuller & Michael Hattaway, eds. *The Cambridge Companion to English Renaissance Drama* (Cambridge University Press, 1990)
Very useful essays on plays and theatre practice between 1580 and 1640.

Peter Brook *The Empty Space* (Touchstone, 1995)
First published in 1968, Brook's views on varieties of theatre (Deadly, Holy, Rough and Immediate) have influenced directors ever since.

Alan Dessen *A Dictionary of Stage Directions in English Drama, 1580–1642* (Cambridge University Press, new edn. 2001)
A unique dictionary, defining and explaining stage directions used before during and after Shakespeare's career.

Christine Dymkowski, ed. *The Tempest* (*Shakespeare in Production* series) (Cambridge University Press, 2000)
The first book dedicated to the stage history of *The Tempest*. A valuable survey of the history of productions of this play, spanning several centuries and many countries.

Andrew Gurr *The Shakespearean Stage 1574–1642* (Cambridge University Press, 1990)
A detailed account of theatre conditions, including much documentary evidence in memoirs, letters and inventories.

Michael Hattaway *Elizabethan Popular Theatre* (Cambridge University Press, 1982)
A concise account of theatre practice in Shakespeare's time.

Pauline Kiernan *Staging Shakespeare at the New Globe* (Palgrave Macmillan, 1999)
How the Southwark Globe was built, the principles that created it and an account of its first year.

Jan Kott *Shakespeare Our Contemporary* (Methuen, 1967)
Kott interprets the plays in terms of 20th-century violence and repression. His harsh political views have influenced many political productions of Shakespeare.

Jonathan Miller *Subsequent Performances* (Faber, 1987)
An important figure in later 20th-century British theatre, Miller discusses the 'afterlife' of Shakespeare's plays and analyses his own approaches to directing Shakespeare on stage.

Stephen Orgel, ed. *The Tempest* (*Oxford World's Classics* series, Oxford University Press, 1998)
An edition of the play by a distinguished American scholar; contains a wide-ranging introduction, discussing the play in the historical and political context of Renaissance literature.

Marvin Rosenberg *The Masks of Macbeth* and *The Masks of King Lear* (University of California, 1978)
Extremely thorough scene-by-scene account of the plays, with illustration and analysis of performances.

James Shapiro *1599* (Faber, 2005)
Shakespeare as an actor, businessman and playwright explored through a crucial year in history and his creative development.

Emma Smith *The Cambridge Introduction to Shakespeare* (Cambridge University Press, 2005)
Accessible and lively insight into Shakespeare, including sections on his writing for performance.

J.L. Styan *Shakespeare's Stagecraft* (Cambridge University Press, 1967)
Follows Granville Barker in exploring Shakespeare's stagecraft and how the conditions of the public playhouses influenced his writing.

J.L. Styan *The Shakespeare Revolution* (Cambridge University Press, 1977)
Shakespeare performance and criticism in the 20th century, from William Poel to Peter Brook.

Stanley Wells *Shakespeare in the Theatre: An Anthology of Criticism* (Oxford University Press, 1997)
Useful source of theatre reviews, showing different values in how Shakespeare has been received.

Stanley Wells, ed. *Cambridge Companion to Shakespeare Studies* (Cambridge University Press, 1986)
A series of essays on the study of Shakespeare, including several on the history of staging his plays.

Stanley Wells & Sarah Stanton, eds. *Cambridge Companion to Shakespeare on Stage* (Cambridge University Press, 2002)
A collection of essays on the history of Shakespeare's plays on stage.

Films, videos and websites

Videos and DVDs of the major Shakespeare plays are available in bookshops and libraries. For some plays (e.g. *Hamlet, Macbeth*) several different versions are available, allowing you to compare different stagings of the same speech or scene.

A useful list of Shakespeare films and videos is in Cathy Grant *As You Like It* (British Universities Film and Video Council 1992; website: www.BUFVC.ac.uk).

Valuable information about plays currently in performance or archive material may be found on:
>
> Royal Shakespeare Company: www.rsc.org.uk
> Shakespeare's Globe: www.shakespeares-globe.org
> The Shakespeare Centre: shakespeare.org.uk
> The National Theatre: www.nationaltheatre.org.uk
> Cheek by Jowl Theatre Company: www.cheekbyjowl.com

Reviews of recent productions may be found by searching online versions of newspapers. In the UK the following do not currently charge for access to their Internet archives:
>
> *The Guardian* www.guardian.co.uk
> *The Independent* www.independent.co.uk
> *The Daily Telegraph* www.telegraph.co.uk

Glossary

Allegory an extended metaphor in which a story or description carries a half-hidden meaning, usually moral or religious. It therefore works on two related levels, as with Spenser's *The Faerie Queen* and Bunyan's *A Pilgrim's Progress*.

Antithesis a type of rhetoric that balances a word or phrase against another. Brackenbury in *Richard III* uses antithesis to stress the difficulties of being royal: 'Princes have but their titles for their glories, / An outward honour for an inward toil.'

Bowdlerise to edit Shakespeare to remove all language, chiefly sexual, that might offend or embarrass a respectable 19th-century family. From Thomas Bowdler's *A Family Shakespeare* (1818).

Caricature exaggerating a character's appearance or behaviour to amuse or make a satirical point. The word came from the Italian 'caricatura', an artist's term for a comic drawing. It was then used for characters in novels and plays. Pistol in *Henry IV* is a caricature of a braggart, and Le Beau in *As You Like It* is often caricatured as an effeminate courtier.

Chorus in some of Shakespeare's plays, a single speaker who takes no part in the action but introduces changes of scene and helps create atmosphere. See, in particular, *Henry V*.

Chronicle Plays the Elizabethan term for plays about history, especially English or Roman.

Decorum appropriateness. 'Decorum' may be used in the context of polite social manners, but in literature it means that a writer chooses the appropriate style of language to fit the subject matter. A tragedy about kings and princes demands a higher style than a comedy about the lower social classes. Verse was thought to dignify an epic or tragedy; prose was more common in comedy.

Didactic from the Latin word meaning 'to teach'. Literature was expected to give moral instruction and to improve behaviour. Stories were 'didactic' if their message was declared directly as in preaching. Plays were often attacked for immorality, but their supporters often defended the teaching values of stories which punished the wicked and exposed immoral behaviour (especially among the upper classes).

Downstage see **Upstage/downstage**

Extempore from the Latin meaning 'out of the moment', therefore unprepared and, in terms of performance, unrehearsed. Elizabethan clowns were skilled at instant inventions of wit and physical comic behaviour.

Farce derived from actors' improvisations in medieval popular comedy. It came to mean a type of lively physical comedy with split-second timing, absurd coincidences and mistaken identity. Ben Jonson's farce *The Alchemist* (1610) continues to be revived. A popular sitcom farce on TV was John Cleese's hotel comedy, *Fawlty Towers*.

Humours the term comes from Greek medical theory which believed that the body's health is controlled by a balance of fluids. From this, 'humours' accounted for personality, so that a type of person might be, for example, 'sanguine', 'choleric', 'phlegmatic' or 'melancholic'. In the theatre the Comedy of Humours contains stereotype characters, each based on a distinct type of personality, and therefore often a caricature (see above).

Iambic a two-syllable foot of verse which, repeated, forms the iambic pentameter, the most frequent form of verse in English poetry and verse drama. At its most regular, the iambic pentameter is a line of ten syllables, alternating unstressed and stressed syllables:

> But I that am not shaped for sportive tricks
> Nor made to court an amorous looking-glass
> *(Richard III Act 1 Scene 1: lines 14–15)*

Most of Shakespeare's blank verse is written in iambic pentameter (as is much of his rhyming verse), but the lively expressiveness of his writing depends much on the slight variants from this regular pattern.

Irony words spoken to a double audience, one of which understands the surface meaning and another which understands more. In *King Lear* Edmund tricks his brother Edgar into thinking his life is in danger. Edgar searches for an explanation, saying 'Some villain hath done me wrong.' Edmund pretends to sympathise: 'That's my fear.' The audience appreciates both meanings: what Edgar understands and what Edmund intends. In this and many other examples, irony can convey a grim comedy.

Machiavel a villainous but witty and entertaining character-type who despises conscience and morality for restraining political ambition. 'Machiavel' acts as the Chorus for Marlowe's *The Jew of Malta*. Richard III, Shakespeare's first machiavel, describes his methods, 'Plots have I laid, inductions dangerous', and boasts that he is 'subtle, false and treacherous'. The term derives from the Italian political theorist Niccolò Machiavelli (1469–1527), who wrote *The Prince* to explain how to achieve and retain power.

Malcontent a character type in Elizabethan and Jacobean tragedy. A discontented man, who may also be a machiavel. Bosola, in Webster's *The Duchess of Malfi*, is a malcontent opportunist who wishes to improve his social status. Hamlet, the prince, is a malcontent commentator on the corruption of the world around him. John Marston's *The Malcontent* was a popular tragic-comedy first performed in 1602.

Masque expensive musical entertainments performed by amateurs at court. Masques depend on lavish spectacle through costume and elaborate scenery. They tell allegorical stories, often in pastoral settings, with moral and/or political meanings, often with gracious tributes to the aristocracy. The most famous Jacobean collaboration was between the poet Ben Jonson and the architect Inigo Jones.

Method acting an attempt to make acting as close as possible to real life, whereby actors draw on emotions, experiences and thoughts from their own lives. It derived from Stanislavski's work at The Moscow Arts Theatre around 1900 and was turned into a 'method' by the director Lee Strasburg in New York in the 1940s.

Neo-classicism an attitude to the arts in the late 17th and 18th centuries which agreed on the pre-eminence of the classical works (chiefly of Greece and Rome) and required those standards of taste and craftsmanship to be upheld by each new ('neo-') generation. Ideally, this meant not slavish imitation but conforming to ancient values.

Proscenium literally, from the Greek, the front part of the stage. In theatres from 1660 onwards the proscenium arch divides the auditorium from the stage. Like a picture frame, it encloses the gap (or removed fourth wall) through which the audience watches the play. The proscenium stage is ideal for opera and other performances that aim for spectacular effects and scenic illusion.

Puritans in 16th- and 17th-century England 'Puritan' was often used as a term of abuse for anyone seeking 'purity' of doctrine and worship outside the established Church of England. They believed in the 'priesthood' of all believers and opposed the 'tyranny' of bishops. The King James Bible of 1611 was an attempt to accommodate their beliefs into the established Church, but their anti-authority influence eventually contributed to the death of Charles I in 1649. Puritans aimed to root out vanity and frivolous behaviour that might encourage immorality; they were therefore hostile to the theatre and to players. Their influence came to an end with the Restoration of Charles II in 1660.

Renaissance literally a 'rebirth' of intellectual and artistic life. It is impossible to date the Renaissance period exactly, but it spread from Italy (especially Florence) throughout Europe between 1400 and 1650. It included the rediscovery of classical learning, the development of science and the growth of patronage of the arts by noble families.

Restoration the English monarchy was restored in 1660 when Charles II came to the throne after 11 years of Puritan rule during the Commonwealth (1649–1660). The term 'Restoration' is often applied to culture and art, especially drama, between 1660 and 1700.

Revenge tragedy a popular type of tragedy in which the plot is driven by a main character's desire to avenge a wrong, usually to his family. Act 5 is usually a bloodthirsty series of events that fulfils his aim. In *Hamlet* there are three of these 'heroes': Hamlet, Laertes and Fortinbras.

Rhetoric an important branch of study in medieval and Elizabethan education, rhetoric is the art of persuasion through language. In modern times 'rhetoric' has become a negative label for empty and pretentious language, especially in public speeches by politicians.

Romance originally stories in Latin ('in the Roman language'), developing into Old French 'roman', romances were courtly stories about knights and ladies, noble quests, fantastical events, often involving magic and mythical characters. Some of Shakespeare's comedies are based on old romances, as are his final plays, *Pericles, Cymbeline* and *The Winter's Tale*.

Romanticism partly a reaction against the formal, classical, rationalistic attitudes that had dominated European arts and literature during the 18th century, Romanticism stressed the importance of the imagination, of the emotional and the irrational; it privileged the individual (especially the outsider) over society. Thus Hamlet could easily come to be seen as a type of Romantic hero, and the storm scenes in *King Lear* (evoking 'sublime' emotions of pity and terror) could appeal to a Romantic imagination. 'Romantic' derives from the term 'Romance' (see above).

Stagecraft the techniques required by writers, directors and actors for creating and communicating plays on stage.

Theme the topic or issue on which a play or other piece of writing is based. Love is one of the themes in *As You Like It* and *Othello*; principles of government in *Measure for Measure*; nature versus nurture in *The Tempest*.

Upstage/downstage terms to describe an actor's position on stage in relation to the audience. Upstage is further away at the back of the stage; downstage is forward and close to the audience. (These terms apply better to a proscenium stage than to a thrust stage where the audience surrounds the actors on three sides.) Soliloquies will always be played downstage. To upstage someone is to distract the audience's attention from another actor by walking behind him or her and then speaking to them, forcing that actor to turn his or her back to the audience, while the person speaking can be clearly seen. actor-managers 55–6, 66

Index